Testifying Under Oath

How to Be an Effective Witness

D1600534

Testifying Under Oath

How to Be an Effective Witness

41 Tips to Prepare You for Court

JAMES M. VUKELIC

VOLCANO
· PRESS ·

Volcano, California

Testifying Under Oath: How to Be an Effective Witness

Copyright © 2005 by James M. Vukelic

All rights reserved. No part of this book may be copied or reproduced by any means, electronic or mechanical, including photocopying, recording, or by any information storage and retrieval system, without prior permission in writing by the publisher.

Library of Congress Cataloging-in-Publication Data

Vukelic, James M., 1950-
  Testifying under oath : how to be an effective witness / by James M. Vukelic.— 1st American pbk. ed.
      p.   cm.
  ISBN 1-884244-26-2 (Paperback)
  1. Witnesses--United States--Popular works. I. Title.
  KF8950.Z9V85 2003
  347.73'66--dc21

                        2003004635

Cover design and illustration by Diane McIntosh
Interior page design by Jeff Brandenburg/image-comp.com

www.volcanopress.com
800-879-9636
E-mail: sales@volcanopress.com

Volcano Press
P.O. Box 270
Volcano, California 95689

Telephone: 209.296.7989
Fax: 209.296.4995

Inquire about bulk discounts

First printing, Volcano Press, Inc. 2005
Printed in the United States of America

About the Author

JAMES M. VUKELIC is a former trial court judge, now serving as the Chief Prosecutor for the Standing Rock Sioux Tribe. He has more than 25 years of courtroom experience as a prosecutor, judge, and civil attorney.

Raised in rural North Dakota, Vukelic learned to operate farm machinery, erect steel buildings, lay concrete, paint houses, bake pizzas, and bartend as he worked his way through school. He earned his bachelor's, master's, and law degrees from the University of North Dakota.

Vukelic is a former high school teacher and guidance counselor. He is a frequent lecturer and trainer in the areas of courtroom testimony and domestic violence.

In his spare time, Vukelic enjoys singing with a barbershop quartet, digital photography, and sports. He and his wife Pam have two grown children, Reed and Meredith. They make their home in Bismarck, North Dakota.

Table of Contents

From the Publishers

When James Vukelic approached Volcano Press with his proposal for TES-TIFYING UNDER OATH, we immediately recognized the great need for a book on this subject.

There are so many reasons why you may be called to be a witness and need to appear in court. You may have observed an event, or you may be bringing your own legal action. You may be called to give testimony by either the defense or the prosecution in a case.

In both factual and yet easy-to-read fashion, author Vukelic offers significant tips about how to be an effective witness, while providing you with anecdotes and sample dialogues that take place in court.

Please let us know if TESTIFYING UNDER OATH has been helpful to you, and if you have any comments.

Ruth Gottstein, Publisher
Adam Gottstein, Associate Publisher
2005

Volcano Press
P.O. Box 270
Volcano, California 95689

sales@volcanopress.com
800.879.9636

Foreword

Often during my years sitting on the bench as a trial judge, I would see a witness struggling to communicate with me or the jury. And within our adversarial court system, there can be intense pressure on a witness, beyond the strange customs and language of the courtroom.

This book is a way to help witnesses testify calmly and persuasively in court. It is designed to familiarize them with the complexities of the trial process and to reduce their anxiety in court.

Most folks are terrified at the prospect of taking the witness stand. Even a seasoned trial veteran will admit that being questioned by a quick-witted, sharp-tongued trial attorney can be unpleasant and challenging. While anxiety is natural and expected, it can interfere with the primary objective of a trial: to reach the truth. If a witness is too nervous to communicate effectively, valuable information that should be presented to the judge or jury may never be revealed.

When witnesses fail to present evidence adequately, the quality of the judicial system suffers and the confidence placed in it by the public is diminished. As a society, we have worked hard to establish, maintain, and improve our court system. While imperfect, our system is able to resolve conflicts and maintain an ordered society, while protecting rights.

My intention in writing this book is to:

- help witnesses testify more effectively
- take the mystery out of court proceedings
- offer concrete advice on how to be a persuasive witness
- expose tricks and traps used by attorneys
- offer ways of dealing with tricks and traps

I include numerous examples to demonstrate key points, many of them taken from real trials. A short history of trials appears in the appendix. Also, look at the glossary at the end of the book for definitions of court terms used here.

By explaining court proceedings and attorneys' methods, this book will enable witnesses to help a judge or jury reach the right decision. That, in turn, can only enhance the judicial system and benefit society.

CHAPTER ONE

What You Need to Understand Before Trial

A trial is still an ordeal by battle. For the broadsword, there is the weight of evidence; for the battle-ax, the force of logic; for the sharp spear, the blazing gleam of truth; for the rapier, the quick and flashing knife of wit.

—Lloyd Paul Stryker

A trial is essentially a battle. Opponents do not fight to the death, but modern dispute resolution in court is nevertheless a form of warfare. Instead of using sticks or swords, we fight in court with witnesses and exhibits. Hired attorneys joust with words and pictures as their weapons.

The premise underpinning our trial procedures is that two evenly matched adversaries will bring out the strengths of their own cause and the weaknesses of the other's. It is hoped that this adversarial system will illuminate the truth for the finder-of-fact, whether that be a judge or jury.

Regardless of how competent you appear as a witness, how unbiased and impartial your view of the case, you will be treated by one side as a comrade and by the other as an adversary. The simple truth is that your testimony helps one side and hurts the other. If this were not so, you would not be called to testify in the first place. If you do not fully appreciate this battleground for what it is, you may be surprised or affronted when you take the witness stand. To be forewarned is to be forearmed.

Making Your Testimony Count

The objective of this book is to increase the odds that your testimony will be well received by the judge or jury. To accomplish this, you must be able to help the judge or jury to understand and accept your point of view.

Like it or not, you will probably become emotionally invested in the process, and even the outcome of the trial. You will want to win. You will want your testimony to be accepted as factual and truthful. You will want to be viewed as a credible person.

When you testify, your credibility is at stake. Indeed, your credibility is one of the targets for the opposing counsel. This usually takes the form of attacking your perception, knowledge of the facts, any bias or prejudice you may have, or your recollection of the events. These modes of attack, or impeachment as it is called in court, will be discussed later at greater length.

The courtroom is a stressful arena. Psychologists have long identified the reaction to stressful situations as the "flight-or-fight response." When faced with acute stress, the heart beats faster, the digestive system slows or shuts down so more blood can flow to the arms and legs, and adrenalin level increases. We gear up to fight or skedaddle, just as our ancestors did when faced with saber-toothed tigers and other menaces.

Even veterans of many trials admit that they experience anxiety — sometimes severe anxiety. Part of that is created by the atmosphere: a room devoid of personality and warmth, a stern-looking judge in a black robe peering down at you from on high, and an opposing attorney poised to attack every word you utter in pursuit of her client's cause. While this atmosphere is not the reality in every courtroom, it occurs frequently enough to cause anxiety.

Unfortunately, there is no opportunity for "flight." Witnesses usually come to court under subpoena, meaning they must attend or be declared in contempt of court. The alternative is to "fight." Although no physical altercation is anticipated, a battle of wits may ensue between the witness and opposing counsel.

How the Legal Process Works

There are two kinds of cases: criminal and civil. In criminal cases, the accused is brought to court in answer to *charges* filed by the *prosecutor*. In all cases, the plaintiff is the party bringing the legal action. The defendant is the one against whom the legal complaint is lodged. A prosecutor represents a governmental body: federal, state, or local. Whether an assistant district attorney, county prosecutor, or city attorney, the prosecutor is typically said to represent the people of that jurisdiction, which is why criminal cases have titles like "People of Idaho Versus John Doe."

In criminal cases, the verdict results in a conviction or an acquittal. If the defendant is acquitted, the matter is ended, since our state and federal constitutions prohibit repeated prosecutions for the same offense. If convicted, the defendant faces incarceration, fines, or other measures intended to rehabilitate or punish.

In civil cases, the most frequent objective of the plaintiff is to recover money (often referred to as damages) for a wrong committed by the defendant, or for an injury suffered because of the defendant's conduct. Some civil actions are not filed to win damages, such as divorces, child custody disputes, and petitions for protection or restraining orders.

Whether the case is criminal or civil, it may be decided by a judge (called a bench trial) or by a jury (jury trial). In both cases, formal testimony is taken under oath and the same *rules of evidence* apply.

A major distinction between civil and criminal cases involves the burden of proof. In civil cases, the plaintiff must prove he or she is entitled to win by a "preponderance of the evidence." This means the plaintiff must show it is more likely than not that certain facts are true. Some attorneys will use percentages to express this concept and tell juries that if they believe the evidence was 51 percent in support of the fact and 49 percent opposed, the jury must then find that the fact has been successfully proven. In criminal cases, however, the prosecution must prove the defendant's guilt beyond a reasonable doubt. Though there are no percentage equivalents, everyone concedes that this burden is much higher than in civil cases.

Most cases, whether criminal or civil, settle out before trial. In the criminal arena, more than 90 percent of all cases are disposed of through a plea of guilty, a negotiated plea agreement, or rarely, with a dismissal of the charge. In civil cases, the percentage is similarly high. Settlements in civil cases typically involve an agreement by the parties to exchange an agreed-upon sum of money in return for dismissing the lawsuit. In the conduct of civil lawsuits today, a lot of pre-trial work is done by the opposing parties. They find out as much as they can about the strengths and weaknesses of a claim, often before the case is even filed in court. When such investigation is done after the case is filed, it is referred to as *discovery*.

The most common methods of conducting discovery, in both civil and criminal cases, are to send a list of questions, or interrogatories, to the other side, and to conduct depositions. A *deposition* is the taking of testimony under oath, but outside the trial setting. You can find more information about depositions in Chapter Six.

Almost all trials, criminal or civil, are heard by juries, rather than by judges sitting without a jury. There are many reasons for this. In the criminal context, judges are generally perceived by the defense attorneys as too conservative, too unwilling to accept a defense they've seen presented countless times before. One judge, during a break in a driving-under-the influence (DUI) jury trial, said, "If I hear the trick-knee excuse for failing the walk-the-line test one more time, I'm going to be sick." In civil cases, plaintiffs typically believe a jury will award them more money in damages than will a judge.

In most cases, you will be attempting to persuade a jury, as the finder-of-fact. But even in jury cases, you will need to impress the judge with your credibility, as it often impacts crucial rulings during trial. Most of the tips relating to nonverbal and verbal persuasion in the following chapters apply whether your target audience is a jury or the judge, and regardless of whether your testimony is given during a deposition or in court.

Just the Facts, Ma'am

It is recognized that you may not have an attorney who specifically represents you in the case. More likely, you will be called by one side or the other to bolster a claim or defense raised by one of them. There will almost always be an attorney you would more closely align yourself with, given a choice. Throughout this book, this attorney is referred to as "your attorney." The other party's attorney is referred to as "opposing counsel."

The attorney who calls a witness to the stand does the direct examination of that witness. The questioning is typically open-ended and not suggestive. The most frequently heard question on direct examination is, "What happened next?"

After your attorney finishes direct examination, opposing counsel conducts what is called cross-examination. On cross-examination, the questioner typically states the facts and merely asks the witness to confirm them. Many questions on cross-examination begin, "Isn't it true that . . . ?" or "Would you admit that . . . ?" An adage repeated by trial attorneys is that you never ask a question on cross-examination for which you do not already know the answer.

The attorney who violates this rule tempts fate, as demonstrated by the following story which has made the rounds among trial attorneys:

CROSS-EXAMINER: So you say my client, Mr. Angel, assaulted Mr. Smith.

WITNESS: Yes, that's right.

CROSS-EXAMINER: And you say my client did this by biting off Mr. Smith's ear?

WITNESS: *Correct.*

CROSS-EXAMINER: But you admit, don't you, that at the same time this alleged assault took place, a train went by within fifty feet of where you were standing?

WITNESS: *Yes, that's true.*

CROSS-EXAMINER: And you admit you were distracted by the train, correct?

WITNESS: *Yes.*

CROSS-EXAMINER: In fact, at the exact moment the alleged assault took place, you weren't even looking at my client, were you?

WITNESS: *No, I wasn't.*

CROSS-EXAMINER: Nor were you looking at Mr. Smith at that time, correct?

WITNESS: *That's right.*

CROSS-EXAMINER: So you couldn't possibly have seen my client commit this so-called assault, could you?

WITNESS: *No, I guess I couldn't.*

(Then comes the question for which the cross-examiner does not know the answer, and should never have asked.)

CROSS-EXAMINER: Without committing perjury, how can you possibly testify under oath that my client bit off Mr. Smith's ear?

WITNESS: *I saw him spit it out.*

After cross-examination, your attorney is allowed to ask more questions but is limited to the areas covered by opposing counsel on cross-examination; this is called redirect examination. At the judge's discretion, there may follow recross-examination, re-redirect, and so on. The only restriction is that the topics covered must be only those just addressed by the previous examiner. In other words, the cross-examiner cannot wait until recross-examination to bring up a new subject which wasn't covered on redirect examination.

In most cases, you should not need to take notes with you to the witness stand. Instead, before coming to court take time to read through your file if you have one and familiarize yourself again with the facts of the case. If you can't testify to the most elementary facts without referring to your notes, you send the judge and jury one of two messages: your memory is too poor to be dependable, or you really don't care much about the matter at hand. Either message may affect the impact of your testimony. See Tip #21 for more discussion on this.

When you have a report, one way of increasing your knowledge of the facts is to have a co-worker, spouse, or friend review it to clarify the issues or areas most likely to be explored and discuss it with you. Probably the best reviewer and advisor in this regard is your attorney.

If the adversarial system is working as intended, any relevant facts you have will be brought to light by one attorney or the other. The better you know the facts, the shorter will be your stay on the witness stand.

Educating Your Attorney

What an attorney does not know can hurt the case. Trial attorneys tell numerous stories of how they were ambushed in the courtroom by the revelation of some fact previously unknown to them. This occurrence is so common that law school trial advocacy instructors advise students of the importance of appearing nonchalant when the bombshell explodes in open court. "Whatever you do," they instruct, "don't appear to be surprised or flustered by the revelation. That emphasizes its importance to the jury. Pretend it was insignificant and hope for the best."

TIP 1

Let your attorney know what you know

Your attorney may have a good idea of what kind of defense the other side will use, and will prepare for it. What no attorney can prepare for are those facts that you know, but have not divulged. There are many reasons why witnesses may choose not to tell the attorney everything they know about a particular event. The most common is the belief that the information will hurt the case and is better left unstated.

Concealing information is particularly dangerous and is unlikely to succeed. Under modern rules of discovery, the opposing attorney is likely to uncover the harmful evidence unless people dishonestly cover it up. Even then, over time, the truth is likely to be revealed. When this happens, opposing counsel can seek a new trial, alleging newly discovered evidence.

If concealment backfires and the undisclosed evidence is uncovered at trial, there is little time to lessen its impact or contradict it. Most trials are relatively short. (Many judges and attorneys, from every state except California, were incredulous that the O. J. Simpson trial took nearly a year to complete.) Murder trials in most states seldom last longer than two or three weeks. In such a short time, a single dramatic revelation is easily remembered at trial's end when the jury begins its deliberation.

When I lecture peace officer trainees, I often cite the following example of harmful information that, if undisclosed, could make or break a case.

Around ten o'clock on a warm summer morning in rural Dunn County, North Dakota, a Native American, Eddie Goodbird, walked into a saloon. Eddie was a regular at the tavern and asked the bar owner, Marvin Wiedrich, if there were any odd jobs Eddie could do to earn some cash.

Marvin, a grizzled fifty-five-year-old, replied that his lawn needed mowing. His yard was just across the alley and Eddie accepted the offer. A short while later, Eddie returned to the tavern and Marvin set him up with a couple of beers. Then Marvin looked across the alley and noticed the yard wasn't completely mowed. He confronted Eddie about this, and an argument ensued. The only other customers, a couple of barflies, immediately left the premises.

Soon, Dunn County Sheriff Larry Boepple received a telephone call from the bar. Marvin reported that he had been attacked by Eddie and had killed him in self-defense. Upon arrival at the scene Sheriff Boepple noticed some welts on Marvin's face and found Eddie lying on his back behind the bar. Two bullets had entered his abdominal cavity. An autopsy determined either shot would have been fatal. It also disclosed Eddie's blood alcohol concentration (BAC) level was .17, almost twice the legal limit. North Dakota had a .10 limit in DUI cases at the time. Many states have adopted a stricter .08 standard.

As a prosecutor, I anticipated the defense would play on any racial animosity held by the jury. Almost all of the prospective jurors were Caucasian, as was the defendant. I figured the defense attorney would subtly work the race angle throughout the trial. He did not disappoint. He thought he had the perfect argument for self-defense before an all-white jury: Marvin was attacked by a drunken Indian. Eddie's BAC was proof positive of his inebriation. It is common knowledge that intoxicated people have lowered inhibitions and are more prone to violence, so the argument went.

Sheriff Boepple made a revelation that allowed us to counter that defense. He told me he'd had a few official contacts with Eddie over the years, that Eddie was not given to violence, and that Eddie was an alcoholic. That last fact could easily have been concealed by the sheriff. One wouldn't usually assume that it could actually help the prosecution.

Yet Sheriff Boepple divulged it and in doing so, I'm convinced, made all the difference in the world to the outcome of the trial.

Knowing Eddie was an alcoholic, I called a toxicologist who testified that for an alcoholic, .17 BAC was normal. Eddie could easily have awakened that morning with a .13 BAC and at .17 would have been no more prone to violence than most people would be at a .04 level. In speaking with jurors after the trial, I learned the toxicologist's testimony was crucial. The defense crumbled. Marvin was convicted. ■

Had Sheriff Boepple kept his "harmful" information to himself, I would not have been able to rebut one of the strongest arguments the defense sought to offer. This demonstrates how essential absolute candor is to good trial preparation.

Witnesses sometimes choose not to "educate" their attorney, erroneously assuming it is unnecessary. Almost all attorneys in the United States earn a bachelor's degree before attending law school. Then there are three more years of rigorous study. Attorneys are a bright group of people. Law schools, however, do not require any particular area of undergraduate study as a prerequisite for admission. Many of my law school classmates majored in political science; others concentrated their studies in such varied subjects as biology, French, theology, and engineering.

Your attorney may know little or nothing about many subjects that you know well. You have expertise by virtue of your experience, education and training. You need to share it with your attorney, as it relates to your testimony. It is far better to be too thorough than to omit something.

Techniques to Reduce Anxiety

Any stress you show in the courtroom can significantly reduce your credibility. You can take several steps beforehand to reduce stress during the trial.

TIP 2

Visit the courtroom

There is no reason why you cannot or should not visit a courtroom before the trial, preferably the one where you will testify later. Go to the courthouse and ask to speak to the court administrator. Explain your purpose and ask for permission to visit the courtroom. Unless it is in use, most court administrators will accommodate you. When you get there, look around. Where is the witness stand? Sometimes witnesses confuse the witness stand with the place where a clerk of court or a court stenographer sits. The witness stand will be the one closest to the jury box. Take your seat there. How easy is it for you to see the judge, the jury box, and the chairs where the attorneys will sit?

In the best of all worlds, your attorney will make the arrangements for your courtroom visit and accompany you. Ask your attorney how the oath is administered to witnesses in this judge's court. Is it done by the bailiff? A clerk? The judge? It can be unnerving to walk into a room full of strangers and not know where to stand, whom to address, or what to do.

If possible, try out the sound system on the witness stand (almost all courtrooms use amplification so witnesses, attorneys, and the judge can be easily heard). If the system is turned off, don't be afraid to walk up to the judge's chair where the sound system controls typically are found. Turn it on.

Adjust your distance from the microphone in order to achieve the desired volume. It is unlikely anyone will fine tune the system during trial to accommodate loud and soft witnesses. Any adjustments must be made by you. Be aware that the microphone may not pick up your voice when you lean back in your chair and that you may come across too loudly if you get too close to the microphone. ■

TIP 3

Understand the chronology of a trial

Ask your attorney what will happen in court on the day you will testify. The course of a typical trial is this:

- Prospective jurors are questioned by the judge and attorneys, and some of them are selected to serve on the jury. Most civil cases have nine jurors, felony criminal cases have twelve jurors, and misdemeanor criminal cases are usually heard by six jurors. The numbers may vary from state to state. The jury selection process is called *voir dire*. It may take anywhere from an hour to several days to complete.

- The judge may give the jury some opening instructions.

- Attorneys make opening statements. The prosecution or plaintiff in a civil case always goes first. The defendant may, but rarely does, reserve opening statement until the plaintiff rests its case (indicating to the judge there are no more witnesses).

- The plaintiff calls witnesses to testify. Each witness is questioned by his or her attorney during direct examination. Almost always, the opposing attorney will question the witness next during cross-examination.

- The plaintiff rests.

- The defendant calls witnesses to testify. The defendant in all criminal cases and in most civil cases is not required to present any evidence nor call a single witness. The burden of proof is always on the plaintiff to prove the defendant has violated the law or is otherwise answerable to the plaintiff's claim. In most criminal cases, the defendant does not testify. In civil cases, the defendant almost always testifies.

- The defendant rests.

- The plaintiff may call rebuttal witnesses.

- The plaintiff again rests.

- The judge may (but is not required to) permit the defendant to present rebuttal evidence.

- Attorneys make closing arguments. The plaintiff argues first and has the right to make a rebuttal argument after the defendant has argued.

- The judge gives closing instructions to the jury. Some judges, by custom or rule, give closing jury instructions before the attorneys make closing arguments.

- The jury retires to deliberate on a verdict.

- The jury returns with a verdict and it is announced in open court.

- In criminal cases, the defendant is acquitted and can leave, or is convicted and may be sentenced immediately or after a pre-sentence investigation has been conducted. ▓

You will want to know if you are coming to court on the same day the jury is selected. You may also want to know if you will be testifying first, last, or somewhere in the middle of the pack. It is hard to generalize about how long you may be required to stay in the courthouse. You may be done in less than an hour, or you could have to spend the whole day. Discuss these matters with your attorney.

TIP 4

Go through a dry run with your attorney

The best preparation you can make for testifying is to have your attorney take you through a dry run. The attorney should put you on the witness stand and ask you the very questions that will be asked at trial, offering a critique as you answer. When done with direct examination, the attorney should assume the role of the cross-examining attorney and ask you questions a defense attorney is likely to ask.

This will give you a good idea of how the interrogation will proceed during the actual trial. It is not only ethical, but you are encouraged to go over your testimony in advance of trial.

Attorneys who are well prepared for trial will have conducted dry runs, or at least given witnesses a list of questions they intend to ask on direct examination. Some attorneys, after interviewing all their witnesses and reviewing pertinent reports, will send each witness a list of questions and anticipated responses to those questions. The list is typically accompanied by a warning that the enclosed responses are based on information previously received from the witness, and that if any of the anticipated responses are incomplete or inaccurate, the witness should contact the attorney to discuss them.

Every attorney has an ethical obligation to refrain from presenting perjured testimony. But attorneys are also required to represent their clients "zealously." This means that, as long as the answers are truthful, attorneys and witnesses are free to rehearse them before trial.

You may have to pester your attorney to give you the necessary time before trial. Ideally, every witness would be prepared to testify by visiting the court room and going through a dry run. In the real world, however, the majority of witnesses are provided little if any time with their attorneys doing these things.

Attorneys are typically very busy people. Unless you are testifying in a significant case, or have a major role in a less significant case, the attorney may not place a high priority on your trial preparation. Be grateful if your attorney spends time just acquainting you with the trial process. ■

TIP 5

Use imagery

Imagery is the process of imagining through any sense: hearing, sight, smell, taste, or touch. Imagery has been used since ancient times as a technique to encourage changes in attitudes, behavior, or physiological reactions. Today it is used in a wide variety of therapies and as a form of meditation. Health care professionals have demonstrated through scientific studies that imagery can affect a number of physiological functions, including brain-wave activity, blood glucose levels, cardiovascular function, gastrointestinal activity, and oxygen supply in tissues.

Coaches have long recognized the importance of imagery, also called *visualization,* in preparing athletes for competition. One swimming coach wrote:

> To perform well in a big meet, you have to "experience" the whole thing in advance! This means you must "feel" the atmosphere of the big occasion, "see" your competitors, the coaches, the pool, and your friends, "smell" the water, "hear" the crowd — I could go on and on, you have to immerse yourself into the entire meet if you want to be truly prepared for it. If you do not do this, you can find yourself becoming overwhelmed on the day by the big occasion. This is exactly what so many swimmers do — they train brilliantly all week and then get stressed out at the meets and do not perform at their best.[1]

A martial arts expert advises his students to do the following:

- Visualize yourself executing a technique with perfect balance, accuracy, and coordination.

- Imagine how to react to a specific self-defense situation. Visualize your opponent or attacker delivering a front kick or right cross. Think about how you should react. See yourself reacting confidently, with strong counters and strikes.

- Create a strong visualization for greater impact. Use all of your senses to observe the detail of sensations, such as the feel and movement of a kick, the texture of your uniform, and the sounds of your feet moving.

- Imagine yourself within your body, rather than looking at yourself from a distance. It creates a more realistic visualization.

- Anticipate the anxiety and stress that comes with competition and promotion testing. Visualize yourself using deep-breathing techniques and performing confidently to reduce your stress level.[2]

All proponents of imagery advise that you begin the process by finding a quiet place to sit or lie down. Successively relax the different groups of muscles by tensing them for five seconds and then letting go. Start with your feet and work your way up the body. By the time you've flexed and released your facial muscles, your body and mind should be more receptive to the imagery exercise.

As with athletic contests, imagine the setting. Yours will not be a swimming pool or gymnasium, but a courtroom. "See" the attorneys, jurors, clerk of court, judge, and perhaps some people in the audience watching the whole thing. Remember the ambiance of the place, the color of the carpet and woodwork. "Hear" the official administer the oath. "Feel" what it's like to sit in the chair on the witness stand, adjusting the microphone, and listening to how your first answer comes across the public address system.

Then imagine yourself being cool, calm, and collected. In your mind, see yourself as an unflappable witness speaking to the jurors as if they were interested neighbors and friends hanging on every word you utter. Visualize a confident, smooth delivery with just the right amount of inflection and a serious tone to your voice. Picture yourself handling cross-examination with measured, matter-of-fact responses. Then see yourself thanking the judge, stepping down from the witness stand and walking confidently out of the courtroom.

There, you've done it! Your body will associate the calm you are experiencing in your resting, imaging setting with the mental environment of the courtroom you have created. Believe it or not, your brain cannot distinguish this dry run from the real thing. If you repeat the imaging exercise, when it comes time to actually testify, you will enter the courtroom with the confidence that you've "been there, done that." Give it a try. It works! ■

CHAPTER TWO

What You Need to Know at Trial

> Judge: You may call your next witness.
> Your attorney: We call Chad Jones.

Nonverbal Persuasion

If you have been seated outside the courtroom, a bailiff or your attorney will call you to take the witness stand. When you enter the courtroom, it may well be the first time the jury and judge see you. This is your one opportunity to make a good first impression. For good or ill, people judge us by our appearance. Assumptions are made about our status and credibility, based solely on how we look. Even though those assumptions and first impressions may be — and often are — wrong, you should not create unnecessary hurdles to your credibility that must be overcome by your testimony.

TIP 6

Prepare yourself physically

Research has shown that maintaining good physical fitness helps ward off disease, builds self-confidence, and reduces stress. These benefits are interrelated and especially important to a witness. If a witness is suffering from a cold or mild flu, it is harder to focus on the questions coming from attorneys. Conveying self-confidence is crucial to establishing credibility. Stress reduction will enhance a witness's comfort level on the stand and bolster self-confidence.

This doesn't mean a witness has to work out for an hour every day. If you already have an exercise regime, stick with it. If not, it is best to start one at least two weeks before trial.

The day of trial may be hectic, but do your utmost to schedule some exercise before testifying. Even if it is a brisk walk around the courthouse a couple of times, it will help clear your mind. Some people like to put on a set of headphones and listen to some soothing music while they walk. Deep breathing exercises may help, too. ■

TIP 7

Avoid excessive jewelry

As a general rule, the less jewelry you wear, the better. If you are married, you should definitely wear a wedding ring, assuming it is not ostentatious. You don't want to blind the jury with the light reflecting from a huge diamond ring. Leave the other rings at home. The same is true for bracelets, necklaces, and earrings. Men should not wear them at all in the courtroom, and women should wear necklaces or earrings only if they do not command attention. Do not wear bracelets on your ankles or wrists.

Be mindful of wearing anything that looks too expensive. Someone on the jury may have a bias against rich people, and be turned off by that beautiful piece of jewelry. Although your role as a witness has some of the trappings of a performance, you should not look like a star. ■

TIP 8

Dress professionally to persuade

At one time, I would have urged witnesses to dress as if they were going to church. But with today's relaxed standards, this is no longer safe advice. I've seen folks in church wearing jeans and tank tops, definitely inappropriate attire for the witness stand.

Anyone who customarily wears a uniform to work should wear it on the witness stand as well. The uniform evokes authority, which is desirable. It is a good idea to have it cleaned and pressed. If your uniform includes a hat, wear it, but remove it as you enter the courtroom. Tuck it under your arm.

If you do not normally wear a uniform, you need to maintain the image of a professional. Psychologist James Rasicot[3] studied the impact of dress on the credibility of witnesses. He had actors recite the same testimony in a mock trial setting while wearing different sets of clothes. He then asked several groups of mock jurors to grade the actors on how believable they were. The results were illuminating: the more conservative the attire, the more authoritative and credible the witness was perceived to be.

For men, the most credible witness was one who wore a dark suit with a white shirt and tie. The least credible witness was one who wore jeans and a T-shirt. Men wearing a sport coat, colored shirt, and tie were viewed as more credible than someone wearing slacks and a sport shirt, but less credible than one wearing a suit. Solid colors or pinstripes are fine; plaids are not. John T. Molloy, in his book, *Dress For Success,* says, "There are only three appropriate colors for men in a business setting — dull, dark and drab."[4]

For women, wearing a suit with a white blouse proved to be the most credibility-enhancing attire. A low-cut neckline connotes someone out to impress with her body, not her mind. A tailored as opposed to loose-fitting look is more authoritative. Solid colors are preferred to mixed, and dark colors are generally preferable to bright ones. Wearing shoes with heels, not spikes, gives an air of sophistication, while wearing flats does not. Women who put their hair up and pull it away from the face look more powerful than those who do not.

For both men and women, wearing glasses connotes you read more and are more intelligent than those who don't wear them. So if you have contact lenses, leave them at home and wear your glasses to court. Shoes should be polished, clothes cleaned and pressed. If you wear a tie, make sure it is of modern width and pattern. You don't have to be a fashion plate or wear the trendiest clothes, but a male witness wearing his grandfather's suspenders and a too-wide, stained tie won't impress anyone. Pretend it's a job interview; you want to make your best impression.

Any hair style, makeup, or clothing that calls attention away from the substance of your testimony should be avoided. You want to make it easy for the jury and judge to concentrate on what you say. ∎

When deciding how to dress, remember that courtroom temperatures often vary. Dress in layers if possible.

TIP 9

Use your entrance to impress

Within the courtroom, all attention shifts to the door when the bailiff exits to summon you to testify. Seconds later you enter and walk to the witness stand. Having visited the courtroom in advance, you know exactly where you're going. You stride confidently to the front of the courtroom and approach the person who administers the oath. In those few seconds, the jury gets its first glimpse of you and immediately the jurors begin to assess your credibility.

What are they looking for as they size you up? Posture and evenness of your gait are two important factors. The advice every mother gives her teenage child is appropriate: "Stand tall, walk erect, and don't slouch." If you walk without hesitation and hold your head high, the jury will see a confident person whom they will immediately respect. You will not disappoint them. ∎

TIP 10

Be prepared to take the oath

The standard oath is, "Do you swear that your testimony will be the truth, the whole truth, and nothing but the truth, so help you God?" There are slight variations in some courts, of course. Some witnesses, generally for religious reasons, prefer not to swear an oath. Most courts will allow an alternative oath along these lines to be given: "Do you promise, under pain of perjury, to tell the truth in these proceedings?" If you want the alternative oath, simply tell the person administering the oath that you prefer "not to swear." They will know what to do.

You should ask your attorney in advance who will be administering the oath to you at trial. It varies from court to court. It may be the judge, a clerk of court, the court reporter, or a bailiff. You can then approach the correct person without having to look to others for direction. This exhibition of courtroom knowledge is likely to impress jurors with your competence.

When you approach the oath administrator, raise your right hand without prompting. Answer the oath query with a firm, audible "I do" or "I will." Then turn and take the witness stand. Before you sit down, it is a good idea to wait for the judge to tell you to be seated. No one will chastise you if you do not, but pausing for a second or two shows the judge and the jury that you respect the judge's authority.

Though many attorneys wish it weren't so, jurors identify with the judge far more often and more closely than they do with any of the attorneys. If there is a disagreement in front of the jury, it is the rare case where jurors side with the attorney. And the judge typically treats the jury with respect. Jurors often see the judge and jury as working together as a team, trying to reach the best decision in the case.

You tap into this natural relationship by showing deference to the judge. Regardless of your personal opinion of the person wearing the black robe, showing courtesy and respect for the position of judge will only enhance your credibility in the eyes of both the judge and jury. ∎

TIP 11

Maintain a powerful posture on the witness stand

James Rasicot also studied the effects of posture on witness credibility. His research again supported mom's advice: "Sit up, don't slouch." In general, Rasicot concluded, the more space you take up when standing or sitting, the more powerful you are perceived as being. Power, he noted, enhances credibility. So, within reason, assume a posture that uses more space rather than less.

Both feet should be on the floor. Arms should be at your side, not draped over the back of the chair or resting with your hands more than a few inches apart. You do not want to give the impression that these proceedings are informal or unimportant. A sprawling appearance tells the jury you lack self-discipline or are insensitive to social norms.

Don't cross your legs or arms. Crossing your legs indicates an informality which is generally foreign to the courtroom. Crossed arms send the signal that you are smug or unwilling to speak openly. Good attorneys will take note of the psychological discomfort that led to the crossed-arms response. It's like waving a red flag at them. As soon as the attorney notes the arms crossing or the body shifting away from the attorney, a question comes immediately to mind: "Why is this person so anxious about this particular subject?" The attorney then silently concludes: "I think this subject is worth exploring further."

Your objective is to keep the opposing counsel's questioning as short and painless as possible. If, through your body language, you prod opposing counsel to keep you on the stand to question you about a subject that evidently causes you anxiety, you may regret it. ■

TIP 12

Don't act like you're lying

Many of us have had the experience of questioning a child about a broken object or some missing cookies. When the youngster's face flushes and the eyes dart, we know the child's response may be something less than truthful.

Ken Lanning is a retired FBI agent who specialized in interrogating criminals. At one of his training sessions, Lanning taught attendees to look for the "indicators of deception" when interviewing suspects. The following list of indicators is representative, though not all-inclusive:

- Rubbing or wringing hands
- Scratching oneself

- Pulling on earlobes or nose
- Stroking or grooming hair
- Inspecting or picking fingernails
- Adjusting clothing
- Taking eyeglasses off or cleaning them
- Picking lint or pulling threads from clothing
- Putting hand to back of head or neck
- Wiping lips or eyes
- Shuffling, tapping, or swinging feet
- Probing ears or nose
- Shifting leg posture or alignment that coincides with pertinent questions
- Wiping sweat
- Locking feet together under the chair
- Turning your body away from the questioner
- Removing or adjusting watches or jewelry
- Drumming fingers rhythmically
- Clutching arms and elbows particularly close to the body
- Hiding mouth or eyes

These deception indicators arise from the unconscious need to relieve anxiety and reduce stress through some movement. When a suspect engages in deceptive conduct, interrogators like Lanning make a note to explore that area in greater detail.

While not all anxiety, especially in a courtroom, is induced by telling a falsehood, most people interpret the stress-reducing behavior as indicative of lying on the stand. If jurors *think* you're lying, it doesn't make much difference whether or not you are testifying truthfully.

Do judges and jurors really know when you're not telling the truth? In some research, judges were accurate only half of the time when guessing which witness statements were truthful and which were fabricated. Another study, however, supports the hypothesis that all of us have a built-in lie detector.

One researcher found that aphasics — people who do not understand the meaning of words but can still communicate because they gather meaning from nonverbal cues — were particularly adept at recognizing lies from the speaker's tone, emphasis, facial expression, and gestures. If aphasics have this ability, the rest of us most probably possess it too, though we may not recognize it.[5] In short, jurors probably have a subconscious feel for whether or not a witness is lying, based on body language and speech inflection. The trouble is, your body language, while indicative of lying, may simply be the result of nervousness.

You need to feel comfortable on the witness stand. That comfort level will rise with experience and with the knowledge of how jurors perceive you. Going through a dry run (Tip #4) and using imagery (Tip #5) will reduce anxiety and lessen the chance that you will unwittingly exhibit indicators of deception. So will learning what to expect in court. ■

TIP 13

Be comfortable with a microphone

Most courtrooms today have sound systems. Jurors with hearing disabilities may be given a special apparatus that allows them to better hear words spoken into the microphones in court. For effective communication, you must use the sound system to your full advantage. If you have the opportunity to visit the courtroom before trial, ask your attorney to turn on the sound system so you can hear how your voice sounds in the room.

If you do not get the opportunity to rehearse with the sound system before trial, calmly sit down, make brief eye contact with the judge and jury, then look to your attorney for the first question. The question almost invariably is: "Would you state your name for the record, please?" As you respond, *listen* to how your voice is amplified and adjust your distance from the microphone accordingly.

Jurors won't mind if the first few words come blasting out at them so long as you move away from the microphone from then on. But if you continually "eat the mike" — speak too closely to the microphone — the loud sound will be abrasive enough that the judge will probably tell you to back away.

A worse problem, and one more frequently encountered, is the soft voice. Women are more likely than men to speak inaudibly on the witness stand, but I've heard testimony from many soft-spoken men who were difficult to understand. Your attorney will usually let you know if you are not coming across loudly enough, but you should be able to gauge this without help. Look at the jury to see if they are following your testimony.

Jurors do not appreciate an attorney constantly advising a witness to speak more loudly. Remember, your words may carry all the wisdom of Solomon, but they will do your cause no good if the jury and judge can't hear them. This is common sense, of course, but the testimony of many witnesses is undervalued because they do not speak up.

A moderately loud voice also indicates confidence. Jurors favor confident witnesses and tend to believe them. ■

TIP 14

Make eye contact

Generally speaking, maintaining eye contact with your listeners is a good method of increasing credibility. It helps establish rapport and assures your audience of your sincerity. Attorneys know this and, if the judge allows it, often stand at the corner of the jury box while questioning an important witness. This requires the witness to look at or in the general direction of the jurors while testifying.

I once prosecuted a divorced father for molesting his five- and six-year-old daughters during a weekend visitation. There was scant physical evidence. The father adamantly denied fondling the girls. Worse, a judge allowed the visitations to continue even after the charges were filed and, sure enough, the girls recanted. In other words, they "changed their story" and told a social worker that the fondling never happened.

This kind of case is a prosecutor's nightmare but I was fortunate to have as one of my witnesses Joan Senzek Solheim. Joan had impeccable credentials as a child psychologist, having been trained at the world-renowned Kempe Children's Center in Denver. She had studied child sexual abuse extensively, and had worked with hundreds of abused children. I wanted her to explain to the jury the phenomenon of "recanting" and what it meant, or rather, what it did not mean.

Joan took the witness stand and looked at me directly as she answered preliminary questions about her education and experience. But when I got to the crucial question, the one that asked her to explain recantation in children, her body shifted. She turned thirty degrees or so in the witness chair so that she was facing the jury directly. Then, with confidence and skill, she looked at each juror in turn as she summarized the professional literature on the topic and explained that children often recant when faced with unpleasant repercussions from their earlier statement. It did *not* mean the sexual abuse did not happen.

Her explanation took three or four minutes. I watched in awe as she nonverbally contacted each juror assuring them of her sincerity. She meant every word she said and she wanted them to know it. They did. I could see that Joan had them eating out of the palm of her hand. When she was done, I wanted to stand up and applaud her, she was so good. The jury convicted.

In another case, a smooth-talking salesman was accused of fraud. He sold coin-operated blood pressure machines, telling customers he would place them in high-traffic areas, and they would reap the profits. The problem was, he sold more machines than he owned. His customers were mostly elderly, naive, and trusting. He bilked them of thousands of dollars.

When the salesman took the stand at trial, he had answers for everything. His attorney must have spent more than two hours asking him questions designed to show the efficacy of the sales scheme. What struck me as odd was that not once, in his two hours of direct examination and twenty minutes on cross-examination, did the defendant look at the jury. Not once. He was a scam artist and I believe the jury spotted him right away. He was convicted after a short deliberation.

There is no rule that says you must look at opposing counsel while being cross-examined. If the question allows you to give anything but a "yes" or "no" answer, you are free to turn to the jury and tell them forthrightly whatever you can honestly say in answer to the query. Pick your moment, though. It looks awkward if you turn to the jury after being asked a question that requires only a brief answer.

Although sustained eye contact is usually viewed favorably by the recipient when judging your credibility, you should be aware that, as in all things human, there are exceptions. For example, numerous researchers have found that among certain segments of the population, eye contact is sometimes viewed as disrespectful or implying arrogance. According to research, this is common in Asian, Pacific Islander, and Native American cultures.[6]

My experience has not borne out this observation among Native Americans. I have seen, talked to, examined, and cross-examined hundreds of Native Americans on the Standing Rock Sioux Tribe Reservation in the Dakotas. Included among them were members of the Lakota, Cheyenne, Mandan, Arikara, Hidatsa, and Chippewa tribes. I have never seen any adverse reaction to solid eye contact. When I have raised the issue with some Native American friends, they uniformly denied there is any stigma attached to normal or sustained eye contact. I caution to add that there are more than five hundred recognized Native American tribes in the United States and my experience may not be universal.

In the end, it is always wise to take your cues from your listener. If you notice a juror avert your eye contact, don't linger and make him or her uncomfortable. Let common sense be your guide. ■

Other Nonverbal Factors That Can Affect Your Credibility

Distractions

You have one chance, and one chance only, to educate the jury. That means you must take advantage of the opportunity by doing everything in your power to keep the jury's attention focused on you throughout your testimony. Anything that distracts jurors from your message will diminish your chances of persuading them.

Things most people find distracting include chewing gum, rattling coins in your pocket, or fumbling with papers in a file while talking. Women should not take a purse to the stand. Men should empty their pockets before going into the courtroom. Leave behind anything that makes noise or is visually distracting to your audience. They need to concentrate on what you are saying and how you are saying it.

Looking at Your Attorney

Although your attorney can help you with adept questioning, as well as objections to some questions put to you by opposing counsel, you are on your own while on the witness stand. Your attorney can't give you hints on how to answer tough questions. So when faced with a particularly hard question from the other side, don't make the mistake of looking to your attorney for help.

If the jury sees this — and they will — your credibility will take a nose dive. Jurors will not trust a witness who can't answer truthfully without assistance. At a minimum, they will infer that you are looking for help because you are unsure of yourself.

Sometimes, you can claim a little breathing room by asking opposing counsel to rephrase the question. "I'm sorry. I don't understand your question. Could you ask it again, please?" or "I'm not sure what you're asking. Could you rephrase your question, please?" If you are polite and the tactic is not abused, you may gain a few precious seconds allowing you time to mentally compose your answer. But if you use the ploy more than once, a jury may see it as an attempt to avoid telling the truth.

Sequestration

"Sequester" is a legal term that means "to keep apart." The sequestration rule is followed in most courts. The gist of it is that if any party wants witnesses kept out of the courtroom until they are called to testify, that party simply needs to ask the judge. The judge will say something like this: "Pursuant to Rule 615 of the Rules of Evidence, I am ordering all witnesses to leave the courtroom and to remain outside until the bailiff calls you. You are also directed not to confer with anyone about the testimony given in this courtroom before such time as you testify yourself."

Your attorney should inform you whether or not the sequestration rule has been invoked, so that you are not surprised when ordered to leave the courtroom. If the rule has not been invoked, you may listen to the testimony given by other witnesses who testify before and after you. Before the trial, it is proper to ask your attorney what other witnesses are expected to say on the witness stand. Yet I recommend *not* listening as other witnesses testify, for reasons I address later.

Even if the sequestration rule is in effect, you are usually permitted to remain in the courtroom while opening statements are made and, generally, it is a good idea to listen while the opposition outlines their theory of the case. But once the first witness takes the stand, I suggest you not be in the courtroom except when testifying. You can catch a blow-by-blow description of the events from your attorney at the end of the day or when the trial is over.

If you are sequestered, most courts hold that you must stay out of the courtroom before *and* after you testify, if there is any chance that you may be called back to the stand as a rebuttal witness. You are free to stay only if your attorney assures the judge that you will not be recalled.

When opposing counsel says, "No further questions, Your Honor," the judge will usually say, "Thank you, Ms. Anderson; you may step down." On occasion, your attorney or opposing counsel will ask the court for permission to recall you as a witness. "Your Honor, I may want to call Ms. Anderson as a rebuttal witness." In this event, the judge will probably advise you that you are still subject to the sequestration rule, meaning that you should not discuss the case with anyone until the trial is over, or until you've been assured you will not be recalled as a witness.

In most cases, when you step down from the witness stand, your part in the trial is completed. So what should you do? I suggest you nod to the judge, say, "Thank you, Your Honor," and walk confidently to the exit. Go out and don't return unless summoned by the court or your attorney. On your way out, avoid eye contact with the attorneys, jurors, or anyone at the counsel table. Do not look to your attorney for verbal or nonverbal cues. If there's information your attorney wants you to have, you'll get it. Any nod or smile exchanged between you will be noticed. Just look straight ahead and leave.

Why not take a seat in the audience? Surely you're interested in the outcome. Even if you weren't, trials can be truly fascinating to watch. Don't succumb to the temptation, because one or more of the jurors will note where you are sitting. Then when another witness makes a bold statement on the stand, jurors may look to you for a reaction. And despite your best intentions, you may convey nonverbally the reaction they're watching for. It can be a lose-lose situation. If you listen to the testimony of someone who, in your opinion, is being less than truthful, and you react nonverbally with a look of disgust, a juror may wonder if you are trying to improperly influence the witness or the jury. If you don't react, another juror may assume you believe the witness's testimony. If you read a book or magazine in the courtroom, jurors will wonder why you are not more interested in the proceedings.

If you are a public employee, some jurors will wonder why you are hanging around a courtroom when you are being paid to do something else. Jurors won't know if you've had to take personal leave from work in order to be in court. I've had jurors tell me they were displeased with a public employee witness who watched the trial after testifying. "I pay taxes to get a day's work for a day's pay. He should have been at work instead of loafing in court." You can't win.

After you leave the courtroom, you don't want to open yourself to criticism or to speculation about your motives. You want to be viewed as someone who is simply relating the facts as they happened, not as a legal vigilante. You need not be concerned that jurors will forget your testimony if you are not visible in the courtroom. During closing argument your attorney will refresh the jury's collective memory regarding the crucial aspects of your testimony.

Feel confident when you leave that you have done your best to convince the jury of the facts. Trust the system to do its job. It will, at least in most cases. Above all, don't look surprised when the judge directs you to leave the courtroom under the sequestration rule, or, worse yet, argue with the judge about your right as a citizen to observe all public proceedings. It has happened. You'll lose.

Jury Observation

A corollary to the advice about sequestration is that you should assume you are always in the jury's view. From the time you circle the courthouse parking lot looking for a space until the time when the jury returns its verdict, you may be noticed by one or more jurors. If two heads are better than one, then twelve sets of eyes perceive much more than most of us imagine. A case of disorderly conduct demonstrates the point (the names have been altered, but the events are real):

Mary Jones worked for an apiarist moving bee hives from field to field. It was hard, physical work and to make matters worse, Mary's boss, George Smith, made unwanted overtures to her and was often rude in his comments to her. George, in his late fifties, was overweight, married, and not attractive to Mary in any way.

One day as they were traveling down a bumpy country road, George made a comment about the firmness of her breasts since they "don't bounce up and down much on this road." To save her job, Mary did her best to ignore him, but a more dramatic incident moved her to take action.

Mary was driving the company truck to work on a sunny morning and pulled down the sun visor to shield her eyes. Something dropped in her lap that almost made her lose control of the vehicle. It was a photograph of a nude, overweight man masturbating in front of a mirror. The photo was cropped at the neck but Mary knew whose body it was. Infuriated, Mary didn't report to work but came to my office to press charges.

I was a county prosecutor at the time. A few months later, George stood trial on a charge of disorderly conduct. During the trial, Mary testified to several incidents of sexual harassment. George took the stand and denied them all. Then George's attorney called George's wife, Patricia, to testify. She told the jury that she and George had been happily married for more than thirty years, had a most satisfactory love life, and that George was not the kind of man who would ever do such things.

I called Mary back to the stand as a rebuttal witness. In the course of that direct examination, Mary said that George had referred to her as Poopsie. Unbeknownst to me at the time, Mary's revelation of the nickname Poopsie must have struck a chord with Patricia. Patricia and George had been seated immediately next to one another at the defense table throughout the trial. I later learned from one of the jurors that George often rested his hand on Patricia's leg, just above the knee. When Patricia heard Mary mention Poopsie, Patricia forcefully took George's hand off her leg and slammed it down on his own thigh. Not a word was spoken, but the jurors, at least several of them, "heard" a message that could not have been clearer.

They convicted George in less than thirty minutes, a record in my county.

In another case, a murderer confessed long before trial and was left with only one defense — insanity. As one of the prosecutors, I distrusted the testimony of the defendant's foster mother, Sunni Day, when she described the defendant as a good, clean-cut young man when he had lived with her. Something about her seemed calculating, but I couldn't put my finger on it.

After the guilty verdict was returned, I followed my customary practice of talking to all of the jurors who were willing to discuss the trial. I believed then, and still do, that to improve your trial skills you need to get an honest critique from someone in the "audience." A juror told me that one day during the trial he had come back to court early from the luncheon recess. There, to his surprise, the defendant and Sunni Day were standing together in a corridor. A deputy sheriff stood nearby. The defendant and Sunni were engaged in a lengthy kiss. It wasn't the sort of embrace typical of a mother and son. The incident only solidified the juror's view that the defendant was an imposter as well as a murderer.

The point is that jurors do not miss much that goes on around them. As a prosecutor, my attention is focused entirely on the witness. Jurors take in much more of their environment.

There are endless opportunities to "bump into" a juror during trial. The longer the trial, the greater the odds this will happen. Even when the jurors are in the jury box and you are outside the courtroom, you cannot assume that your conduct will not make its way back to the jury. Often, a friend or relative of a juror will come to court to observe events. If the court takes a recess, the observation of you made by this friend or relative may later be conveyed to a juror.

Judges routinely admonish jurors not to talk with anyone about the case during recesses or when they go home at night. But take my word for it, the admonition does not prevent information from being exchanged. Most jurors do not deliberately break the rules, but neither do they turn a deaf ear to someone who has a juicy bit of information about the star witness for the prosecution — you! Act accordingly.

Before trial starts, you will likely be subpoenaed to come to the courthouse. You may have to wait while the jury is selected. At this point, no one knows who among the several citizens summoned for jury duty will finally sit on the jury. Everyone you meet in the hall might become a juror.

After *voir dire*, or jury selection, you may encounter a juror returning to the courthouse from lunch. Contrary to popular belief, jurors are seldom forced to stay together outside the courtroom until they begin deliberations.

Examining Exhibits

It is possible — even likely — that you will introduce some exhibit at trial. Without you, that document or object will not become part of the evidence for the judge or jury to consider. Attorneys who want to have an exhibit admitted must first get the judge's authorization. To do this, they usually must lay a proper foundation. If, for example, you wrote a letter and your attorney wants to introduce it into evidence, a proper foundation could be laid through questions about its creation and authenticity.

YOUR ATTORNEY: Your Honor, may I approach the witness?

JUDGE: *Yes, you may.*

YOUR ATTORNEY: Ms. Hernandez, I show you what has been marked for identification as Plaintiff's Exhibit # 13. Do you recognize it?

WITNESS: *Yes, I do.*

YOUR ATTORNEY: Tell us what it is, please.

WITNESS *(after examining item): It is a letter I wrote to the defendant.*

YOUR ATTORNEY: When did you write the letter?

WITNESS: *On December 15 of last year.*

YOUR ATTORNEY: Is that your signature at the bottom of the letter.

WITNESS *(after examining item again): Yes, it is.*

YOUR ATTORNEY: What did you do with the letter after you wrote it?

WITNESS: *I put it in the out basket at work for delivery to the post office.*

> **YOUR ATTORNEY:** Has the letter been altered or changed in any way since you wrote it?
>
> **WITNESS:** *No, it hasn't.*
>
> **YOUR ATTORNEY:** Thank you. Your Honor, I offer Plaintiff's Exhibit # 13.
>
> **OPPOSING COUNSEL:** *No objection, Your Honor.*
>
> **JUDGE:** Exhibit # 13 is admitted.

Be certain, before you say so under oath, that the item is what you think it is. I have presided over cases where witnesses *assumed* exhibits were something other than what they really were. At best, it causes confusion to correct the mistake later and reflects poorly on the witness who did not take the few seconds necessary to examine it. At worst, an exhibit becomes part of the record when it should not have been admitted into evidence.

You may be able to tell at a glance what an exhibit is. Nevertheless, it shows the jury that you are a careful person if you examine it before answering the attorney's question. You are under oath, after all. It reflects well on you for the jury to see that you take your role as a witness seriously.

Examining and Marking Documents

During cross-examination, you will often be asked to look at a document before questions are asked about it. Look it over closely from start to finish. If the attorney quotes a passage from the document, check to see whether it is being taken out of context. If the quote does not reflect the general tenor of the writing, say so.

You may be asked to put some mark, a circle, or initials, on a document, photograph or diagram to indicate the location of a particular thing. If you are at all uncertain about the location, give yourself some latitude by drawing a large circle or "X."

Identifying Another Person in Court

At some point in your testimony, you may be asked to identify the defendant or another person in court. The examination typically goes like this.

> **YOUR ATTORNEY:** Mr. Rogers, the person driving the red car you collided with on March 8, do you see him in this room?
>
> **WITNESS:** *Yes, I do.*
>
> **YOUR ATTORNEY:** Would you point him out please?

WITNESS:	*He's the man in the white shirt and blue tie, sitting at the counsel table next to Attorney Abercrombie.*
YOUR ATTORNEY:	Let the record reflect the witness has identified the defendant.
JUDGE:	*The record will so reflect.*

When you make the identification, use your arm, hand and finger to physically point out the person identified. Use a firm voice and identify the person without hesitation. You are certain of your identification, so let the judge and jury know that. It also makes for a better record if you use words to describe what the person is wearing. "She's wearing the white blouse at the counsel table, sitting next to Attorney Jameson," is better than, "She's the one sitting over there."

On a rare occasion, opposing counsel may attempt to test a witness's ability to correctly identify a defendant by having the defendant sit in the audience next to other people similar in dress and appearance. If for any reason, you are unsure of your ability to identify the defendant, let the your attorney know this immediately.

Requesting a Break

During a hearing or trial, the judge will ordinarily take a ten or fifteen minute recess every ninety minutes or so. There's no hard and fast rule, but judges recognize it is uncomfortable for jurors and others to sit for long periods without a break. An old adage is followed by judges: "The brain can only absorb what the seat will endure."

Nevertheless, it is possible you may be on the witness stand for a long time. If it has been more than an hour, or you need to use the bathroom or have some other reason for a break, ask for one. Simply turn to the judge and politely ask, "Your Honor, I'm really in need of a break. Will we be taking a recess soon?" The judge will likely address opposing counsel (you would not want to interrupt the flow of your attorney's examination unless absolutely necessary) and ask, "Mr. Compton, how long will it take to finish your questioning?" If the response is anything other than "I only have two or three more questions, Your Honor," the judge will likely take a recess immediately. Judges have bladders, too.

If the judge grants a recess, be sure you do not engage in *any* conversation with opposing counsel, unless your attorney is present and has no objection. You are under no obligation to answer any questions put to you when you are not on the witness stand testifying under oath. Attorneys can be cordial or overbearing. They may attempt to cajole you into "clarifying" some matter you just testified about, or they may imply that you are required to talk to them. Do not fall for either ruse. To draw from the Miranda case, "Anything you say can and will be used against you in a court of law."

If you make the slightest admission of anything useful to opposing counsel, rest assured it will be brought out when you return to the witness stand. Remember, you are not going to convince opposing counsel of anything, and even if you do, attorneys are duty-bound to represent their clients' interests. In other words, you have absolutely nothing to gain — and you do have something to lose — by engaging in conversation with opposing counsel.

The same goes for witnesses you know will be testifying on behalf of an opposing party. Anything you say to them will likely be relayed to opposing counsel. If it helps their case, it will be dragged out of you after the recess. It is best to find a room where you can meet with your attorney or simply be away from other participants in the trial. Use the break to relax, unwind a bit, and think about the points you need to make when the questioning resumes.

Effective Use of Visual Aids and Demonstrations

Attorneys are taught that there are two ways of assuring that the jury will remember a key point: repetition and multi-sensory input. Repetition is done by emphasizing the point in the attorney's opening statement, again during examination of the witnesses, and yet again in closing argument. Trial advocacy instructors advise attorneys, "Tell them what you're going to tell them, tell them again, and then tell them what you've told them." If you are going to rely only upon the spoken word to inform and persuade, repetition is often necessary.

Multi-sensory input usually means using visual and auditory methods to make a point. Most evidence at trial is presented through oral testimony. This is only partially effective. Studies have shown that jurors remember much more information if it is presented visually as well as orally.[7] A picture may truly be worth a thousand words.

Some jurors are auditory learners, but they are in the minority. Most people are visual learners. Some simply will not "get it" if facts are presented in only one manner. Any witness will greatly enhance a presentation by offering both auditory and visual components. This takes careful thought and preparation.

Photographs

Photographs are probably used more often than any other visual aid, and for good reason. They tell the story more quickly, and often more reliably, than can be accomplished with verbal description. It is a rare case in which photographs would not enhance the testimony of a witness.

For example, in a dispute over the worth of some personal property such as an automobile, a photograph of it will give the jury or judge a much better idea of the item's condition than the words "dented" or "beat up." In a personal injury action, photographs of the injury or of the vehicles involved in the collision send a strong message that supplements, even supplants, testimony.

Photographs, like all exhibits, must be approved by the judge before a jury will be permitted to view them. Your attorney usually will have sought and gained this approval before trial. A judge can disallow photographs that are unduly prejudicial or irrelevant. Most judges will not keep out photographs that are relevant, but may exclude them if they are gruesome or gory. Nevertheless, in an appropriate case, even horrendous autopsy photos may be admitted.

Although photographs can be taken to the jury room for closer inspection, it is always a good idea to have them *enlarged*. Any photo developer can print the photos on a hard stock that allows them to be handled without tearing or folding. All photos should be at least eight by ten inches. Another good presentation method is for the witness to use very large (18" x 24") photographs on the witness stand while jurors follow along by viewing smaller versions in photo albums prepared for each of them. An additional photo album should be given to the judge.

This latter point is important. Jurors need to see what you're talking about for the photo to have maximum impact. Sometimes attorneys make the mistake of admitting a photo into evidence, correctly asking for permission to present it to the jury for inspection, then continuing to question the witness while the jurors are still passing the photo around the jury box. This is not useful. No one can listen attentively to testimony and examine a photograph at the same time. Additionally, jurors are distracted while the photograph is handed from one to the next. The correct procedure is for the attorney to ask the judge's permission to show the photo to the jury, then wait until all have reviewed it before continuing with the examination.

If your attorney is not adept and starts questioning you before every juror has seen the photograph, you can politely ask, "Do you want to wait until all of them have seen the photograph?" While your attorney may be a little embarrassed, jurors will secretly thank you.

When you are cross-examined, refer back to one of the photographs the jury saw earlier to make your point. "The 'yield' sign was located 100 feet from the place of impact. I believe you can see that on Exhibit #32." If the jurors still have their individual photo albums in their laps, many will instinctively open them to photo #32 as you are speaking. This is powerful reinforcement of a point you made earlier.

If used correctly, photographs can be your best support at trial. Use them to your advantage.

Making a Point Visually

The means and methods of visual demonstrations are limited only by your imagination. The judge has discretion to allow almost any kind of demonstration or to admit any exhibit for demonstration purposes. This is the test the judge uses to decide if an exhibit can be used in court: Will the demonstration or exhibit make it easier for the jury to understand the witness's testimony? The answer is usually, "yes."

You can brainstorm with your attorney and others about what will help. You can use charts, models, mannequins, photographs and maps. You may be permitted to use a slide projector, blackboard, flip chart, or VisCam visual presenter (a computerized overhead projector) to show something to the jury.

> The judge may allow you to conduct an experiment in the courtroom. During one murder trial, a forensic chemist testified about his examination of the murder scene. A young man had been bludgeoned to death while he slept in the defendant's bed. The body was gone when the chemist arrived on the scene, and the walls looked clean but were not.
>
> "I figured the suspect probably wiped the walls down," the chemist told the jury. "I had a chemical reagent with me that would detect the presence of blood. So I sprayed it on that part of the wall where I thought there might be some blood. I then used a fluoroscope to illuminate the area. The presence of blood shows up green under the fluoroscope."
>
> "Would it assist the jury to understand your testimony if you could demonstrate here in court what you did on the night you examined the scene?" the attorney asked. "Yes, it would,"

the chemist answered. Over the defense attorney's objection, the judge allowed them to conduct the experiment.

The chemist took a piece of wallpaper identical to that found at the scene, put a few drops of blood on it, wiped the blood off with a paper towel, then sprayed the chemical reagent on the stained area. The lights in the courtroom were dimmed. The chemist turned on his fluoroscope and shined it on the stained area. It was a highly dramatic moment in the trial. And then, nothing! The blood didn't show at all. The experiment was a complete flop.

––––––––––

There is a lesson here. Never —I repeat — never conduct an experiment in court without first practicing it outside the courtroom.

If you are asked by opposing counsel to participate in a demonstration, be wary. Often, opposing counsel will want you to step down off the stand and show the jury how an event occurred. If you are asked to assume the role of someone other than yourself, be sure to point out differences in your height and weight, strength, or other factors, as you are engaged in the demonstration. "Of course, I am a lot taller and heavier than your client, Mr. Haskell."

If opposing counsel has you demonstrate things in a manner that differs from the actual event, be sure to point it out. *Nothing in the rules says you have to remain quiet during a demonstration.* If opposing counsel gets exasperated with you, she or he may tell you not to speak unless questioned. If that happens, look to the judge and say, "I'll do whatever you require me to do, Your Honor." Then abide by the answer. Remember, *the judge has the authority to control the courtroom or anything that happens inside it;* the attorney does not.

Charts

There are several things to keep in mind when using charts. Most trial attorneys will tell you that an exhibit which appears to have been prepared by a professional will be more persuasive than something that looks homemade. I think it depends on the exhibit. Sometimes a folksy approach is as effective as a more polished one. Consult with your attorney about this. In trial tactics, there are few absolutes.

But here is one of them. *Make sure the chart and all printing on it are large enough to be seen at a distance of twenty feet.* Another good reason to visit the courtroom where the trial will be held is to gauge the distance from the last row of the jury box to the place where you will be using the exhibit. Ask someone to sit in that juror's chair and tell you if the exhibit is visible. If they can't see it, you've wasted a great deal of time and energy preparing it for use at trial.

Unlike photographs, charts often are not admitted as evidence. When jurors retire to deliberate, they can take with them photographs and any other items that have been received into evidence. Since most charts are only used to demonstrate a point, they are not taken into the jury room at the end of the trial. This is another reason why charts must be made in such a way that they can be easily viewed during trial.

Generally speaking, the fewer words printed on a chart or exhibit, the better. Use the exhibit to explain concepts or ideas. Don't try to include the entire exposition in an exhibit. The exhibit enhances your testimony; it is not a substitute for it.

As is true with photographs, you can overdo it with too many charts. Jurors may inwardly groan when you place Chart # 6 on the easel. If your testimony is so difficult to understand that you need several charts to explain it, your case is probably in trouble with a jury and even with some judges. Attorneys are often advised at trial seminars to remember the KISS principle: *Keep It Simple, Stupid*. The easier it is for the jury to understand a subject, the greater the likelihood of winning on that issue.

A witness should *simplify* as much as possible when testifying about difficult or complex matters. Gear your presentation so it will be understood by jurors with a high school education.

When presenting anything on a chart, be sure of two things. First, *talk to the jury*, not to the chart. Sometimes it is helpful to use a pointer instead of your hand or finger to identify something on the chart. Locate it, then turn to your audience, the jury, and say what you have to say. Second, stand to the side of the chart, not anywhere that blocks any juror's view of the chart. This is another good reason to use a pointer. The beautiful chart you labored so hard to prepare is of little value if all of the jurors cannot see it or cannot hear what you have to say about it.

To use charts effectively, you should practice. If you have a patient companion with you on the day you visit the courtroom in advance of trial, ask him or her to listen to your presentation. Then ask for a critique — not so much on the substance of your discourse — but on your delivery and the visibility of the chart.

The Flip Chart or Blackboard

Most courtrooms are equipped with a flip chart or blackboard for a witness to write or draw on. Almost all of us grew up with blackboards in school, but many have never used a flip chart. The flip chart is simply a large tablet of white paper mounted on an easel. You can draw on a sheet with a marking pen. When it is full, tear it off or flip it over the top of the easel, then write on the next sheet.

More often than not, if you are asked to draw something, it will be at the request of opposing counsel. Your attorney would normally prefer that you use a prepared chart or document. Drawing on blackboards or flip charts is usually done for demonstrative purposes. Typically, these are not taken into the jury room when jurors deliberate.

This makes the presentation in the courtroom all the more important. Again, make sure the audience hears what you are saying as you draw. Do not stand in the way of the drawing as you explain it.

Things to keep in mind are geographical directions, size, and descriptions for the record. Maps generally have the direction north on the top of the document and east on the right. To not confuse the jurors, your drawing should comply with these standards.

Remember, *your drawing must be legible to the farthest juror*. That means you have to depict things larger than may seem natural to you. If you print the names of buildings or streets, or if you label vehicles at the scene of a collision, be sure to use large letters. Alternatively, you may use one large letter, "D" for example, to denote the defendant's car. Just be sure to explain this to the jury as you are writing.

Draw on the top two-thirds of the paper only. It is harder for jurors to read the bottom of the page. Seven words fit nicely on one sheet. Things get crowded when you write more than that.

Draw in proportion. If you are asked to draw the intersection where two vehicles collided, don't make a car larger than the street on which it traveled. Think ahead. How will you draw the rooms in a house or a stretch of highway, if those subjects are likely to be covered during your examination?

The record refers to the transcript that will be reviewed by a higher court if there is an appeal of the jury's verdict. When using flip charts and blackboards, be aware that the *appellate court* considering the appeal will not have the benefit of your drawing. The record will include only your words, so be very descriptive with them. Do not use words like "here" and "there" when pointing to your drawing. "The red car was over here" is not helpful to the reader. Instead, say "I'm making an 'X' on the left side of the diagram to show where the red car was located in the ditch on the west side of the road."

Here, again, practice makes perfect. If you have any inkling that you may be called upon to draw the scene and describe an event, get yourself to a courtroom with a friend and try it out before the trial. Ask your "audience" to pay careful attention to the words you use in describing what happened and to give you feedback.

Other Exhibits

Jurors like to see and feel things that are unfamiliar to them. While a particular item you work with daily may be old hat to you, it can enliven your testimony if you use it for a little show-and-tell. This not only captivates your audience, but gives you a golden opportunity to demonstrate your knowledge and expertise.

You may use anything that makes your testimony more easily understood. Brainstorm some ways to enhance your testimony. You are not limited in the number of items you use, assuming the judge allows them. Most will.

If you are keeping the jury interested in your presentation, the judge will likely be interested as well. Judges, more than anyone else, are easily bored. They've heard most everything before, so whatever you can do to liven things up will probably be appreciated — as long as you don't take too much time to conduct your demonstration.

Again, the key is to practice with the object, so that your presentation to the jury will go smoothly. If you properly use an exhibit, you can enhance your credibility in the eyes of the jury.

Some Dos and Don'ts at Trial

TIP 15

Prepare answers to anticipated questions

Good attorneys will want to enhance your credibility with the jury or judge by having you tell something about yourself with which the listener can identify. The questioning may go like this:

YOUR ATTORNEY: Please introduce yourself to the jury.

WITNESS: *My name is Peter Carvell.*

YOUR ATTORNEY: Would you tell us a little about yourself?

WITNESS: *I'm a computer technician with ComputerLand store here in Sacramento. I'm married and we have two grown children. Both my wife and I grew up in California, and we've lived here all our lives. I attended the University of Southern California where I earned my bachelor's degree in computer science. In my spare time, I like to referee softball games and do some fishing.*

There are no blanket rules applicable to this kind of question. Every tidbit of information in your response may resonate with one or more jurors, so it does not hurt to add detail to your narrative. The fact that you are married will be a plus in the minds of most married folks. Parents identify with other parents. Someone on the jury may be an avid softball player or angler. If you are unsure whether or not to include a particular piece of the biographical sketch, ask your attorney for advice. Limit your sketch to thirty seconds and practice it in front of a mirror. ■

TIP 16

Make sure you understand the question

Attorneys have bad days, just like everyone else. Especially when the attorney has not prepared adequately, questions may be unclear. To illustrate, this is an excerpt from an actual trial:

PLAINTIFF'S ATTORNEY: When he went, had you gone and had she, if she wanted to and were able, for the time being excluding all the restraints on her not to go, gone also, would he have brought you, meaning you and she, with him to the station?

DEFENSE ATTORNEY: *Objection. That question should be taken out and shot.*

Sometimes the question refers to earlier testimony but this is clear only in the questioner's mind. For example: "You're saying then, that because they did this, you had to do it, too?" The judge does not expect that you will be able to adequately answer jumbled questions, and the judge wants the matter to be clear for the record. If your attorney objects to the form of the question, the judge will likely sustain (agree with) the objection and ask the interrogator to rephrase. If there is no objection, it is permissible and *advisable* to ask for clarification. "I don't think I understand what you are asking me." Be polite. Don't impugn the skills of the examining attorney, but simply evoke an attitude of wanting to be helpful. "Could you please rephrase that question so I can better understand it?"

Attorneys will sometimes ask a compound question, one which actually contains two questions. Some attorneys ask them deliberately, to confuse the witness or in an attempt to get a concession, but most are simply less careful with their language than they ought to be.

Here is an example: "You have a four-year-old daughter who is very shy, don't you?" A proper response might be: "Yes, I have a four-year-old daughter, but I would not agree about her shyness."

Another example is: "What color was the traffic light and how fast were the two cars going when they got to the intersection?" A good response is, "Could you rephrase that please?" or "I'm sorry, counsel, which part of your question do you want me to answer first?" ■

TIP 17

Do not use profanity

It should go without saying that you should not use profanity while in the courtroom. It's not that the judge and most, if not all, of the jurors haven't done their share of swearing. But there is a strong taboo against conduct that reduces the dignity of court proceedings. The judge, by rule, has the power to punish transgressors on the spot. An attorney who swears in court will probably be fined; the same is true for a witness.

A witness who swears on the stand may get by with only an admonition from the judge, if an apology follows the outburst before the judge has to respond. "Oops! Sorry, Your Honor, that slipped; it won't happen again." But an unrepentant witness is begging for at least a dressing down by the judge. This can't help but diminish the witness's credibility in the eyes of the jury.

There are two exceptions. When a witness is quoting the exact language used by another, it is permissible to swear. If this should arise during your testimony, first turn to the judge and ask permission:

YOUR ATTORNEY: What did Mr. Martin say when you knocked on his door?

OFFICER: *Your Honor, should I use the exact words he used?*

JUDGE: Yes, you may.

OFFICER: *He said, "What the hell do you want? You sons of bitches have been nuthin' but a pain in the ass since you moved into our neighborhood."*

These questions will usually arise on direct examination and you will most likely know ahead of time that the question is coming. So be prepared to ask the judge.

Another time you may use profanity is on cross-examination when you are quoting language you used at an earlier time. Here it is important to be candid. If you used profanity, admit it. If you don't admit it, opposing counsel will exaggerate the issue.

OPPOSING COUNSEL: After you rear-ended my client, and she got out of her car, what was the first thing you said to her?

WITNESS: *I said something like, you shouldn't have stopped so fast. I didn't have a chance to stop.*

OPPOSING COUNSEL: That's not what you really said, is it?

WITNESS: *Something like that; maybe not those exact words.*

OPPOSING COUNSEL: Tell us what you really said.

WITNESS: *I'm not sure I remember the exact words.*

OPPOSING COUNSEL: You used some profanity, didn't you?

WITNESS: *I may have.*

OPPOSING COUNSEL: Come on, now, sir, you called her a dumb bitch, didn't you?

WITNESS: *I could have.*

OPPOSING COUNSEL: You screamed at her, "You dumb bitch, you made me hit you," didn't you?

WITNESS: *I probably did.*

OPPOSING COUNSEL: Were you having trouble controlling your temper that day?

WITNESS: *Not really, no.*

OPPOSING COUNSEL: So that's how you respond to situations where something angers you?

WITNESS: *No.*

OPPOSING COUNSEL: Was something else bothering you when you were driving down the street just before the crash?

WITNESS: *No.*

Opposing counsel can drag this out for quite a while, making the witness increasingly uncomfortable. Worse, it distracts the jury from more important issues. All of this could have been avoided by answering like this:

OPPOSING COUNSEL: After you rear-ended my client, and she got out of her car, what was the first thing you said to her?

WITNESS: *Your Honor, I apologize for using this language in your courtroom. I said, "You dumb bitch, you made me hit you." Ms. Jones (look at her), I'm sorry for swearing at you.*

If you apologized to Ms. Jones before court, make that clear. "Ms. Jones (look at her), I again apologize to you for my conduct. I'm sorry." Not only have you done the right thing by apologizing; now you have disarmed the opposition. When *you* recite the swear words, you can give the language the emphasis you desire. But when opposing counsel quotes you, the inflection and tone will be harsher. The lesson is to *control what you can* while on the witness stand. ■

TIP 18

Do not argue

There will be times when opposing counsel asks questions that seem totally unrelated to the issues before the court. The temptation is to tell opposing counsel to "get with the program" and redirect attention to the matters of importance. I've heard witnesses, in response to cross-examination, admonish the interrogating attorney by saying, "That's irrelevant!"

What follows typically is a request from opposing counsel for the judge to order the witness to answer the question. That is, if the judge hasn't jumped in first and instructed the witness, "I decide what's relevant in here. That's what I get paid to do. Answer the question!" In either case, the witness's attempt to argue with opposing counsel backfires.

It requires a degree of faith, but you have to rely on your attorney to make proper and timely objections to irrelevant or otherwise hostile questions. Many seemingly irrelevant questions are, in fact, relevant. Evidence is relevant if it tends to prove any fact important to the case.

A judge will require a witness to answer questions about relevant facts, even if an objection is raised. For example, questions that challenge a witness's bias or perception are perfectly proper, even though they don't relate to the specific facts of the case. That is so because a witness's bias or problems of perception are almost always important. The bias or inability to correctly perceive events should affect the weight a jury or judge gives to testimony.

Jurors are human. If they see that opposing counsel is "beating up" a witness for no apparent reason, they may hold it against that attorney. Even if they don't, your attorney may choose to make the point in closing argument rather than as an objection during your testimony. "The opposition's case is so weak they spent their time questioning our witnesses about entirely irrelevant matters. They did not challenge the strengths of our case because they could not. That is why they tried to distract you with these details unrelated to the case." So don't get disgusted if your attorney does not object to questions which seem irrelevant. Trust her judgment and roll with it. ■

TIP 19

Speak in your own words

It is important that you use your own words when testifying. If you try to memorize what someone else has written for you, your nonverbal language will give you away. Using a technical or scholarly vocabulary in an effort to impress jurors is bound to backfire, particularly if opposing counsel is adept at exposing it.

This is not to say that you should "dumb down" your language. You may be accustomed to using terminology unfamiliar to the average person. You need not avoid using technical terms so long as you define or explain them immediately.

YOUR ATTORNEY: Ms. Jones, did you have any difficulty getting into the county courthouse?

WITNESS: *Yes. I don't think it is ADA compliant. By that I mean that it doesn't comply with the Americans with Disabilities Act because there was no access for people in wheelchairs.*

Although some people in the courtroom will know that ADA stands for the Americans with Disabilities Act, if one or two jurors do not understand the acronym, important testimony may be lost. As a general rule, avoid jargon, acronyms and abbreviations. ■

TIP 20

Be careful answering "always" or "never" questions

A favorite ploy of cross-examining attorneys is to ask a question, get the anticipated response, then follow with an "always" or "never" question. For example:

ATTORNEY: You don't leave your children home alone, do you?

WITNESS: *No, I don't.*

ATTORNEY: You *never* leave them unattended?

WITNESS: *Right, I don't.*

ATTORNEY: *So if you are away for any reason, you always have a responsible person in the home to watch over them, is that your testimony?*

WITNESS: *Yes.*

Be careful when answering these "always" or "never" questions. In most cases, the attorney has a witness in the wings prepared to testify that the witness did, in fact, do the very thing he or she assured the jury never happened, like having left the children unattended on a particular occasion. Unless you are absolutely certain, it is better to give yourself some leeway.

ATTORNEY: You don't leave your children home alone, do you?

WITNESS: *I can't remember a time when I have.*

ATTORNEY: You *never* leave them unattended?

WITNESS: *I try very hard not to.*

ATTORNEY: That doesn't answer my question. Are you saying that you *always* have a responsible person in the home to watch your children when you're away?

WITNESS: *To the best of my recollection, yes.*

If you believe there exists an exception to your general rule, you could respond like this:

ATTORNEY: You don't leave your children home alone, do you?

WITNESS: *I can't remember a time when I have.*

ATTORNEY: You *never* leave them unattended?

WITNESS: *I may have, but it would have been a very rare occasion.*

ATTORNEY (doing some fishing here): Tell us about those occasions. (Note that the attorney has converted a possible single occasion into the plural.)

WITNESS: *I can't remember a specific time or date when it happened.*

ATTORNEY: But it happened?

WITNESS: *It may have.*

Remember, a witness is sworn to tell the truth. If you remember a specific incident and are asked about it, you must admit it. That does not mean you have to volunteer information that is not asked for. ■

TIP 21

Do not take your notes to the stand

Like Linus in the comic strip *Peanuts*, we all have our security blankets. Some of them are physical, and others are mental tricks we've learned to calm our jangling nerves. Your notes fall into the former category. "I'd be lost on the witness stand without my notes!" several witnesses have told me. Nonsense. You don't need them. Taking them with you to the stand may actually hurt your case.

You cannot persuade someone to believe a set of facts unless you know them well enough to convey them easily. A jury or judge will view the halting, stammering, unsure witness as less credible than another who exudes confidence by demonstrating familiarity with the facts. This may stem from our knowledge of the tendency to stall when we don't know the answer or when we wish to fabricate one. The better you know your facts, the easier it will be to fend off attacks on your credibility.

In most trials, the parties will have found out most everything in the opponent's arsenal before the trial begins. Through the process of discovery the parties can ask for copies of an opponent's reports, results of examinations, and most anything else that will help them defend the case. The attorneys will know which witnesses will testify, and they have a good idea what they will say on the witness stand.

The odds are quite good that the attorneys for both sides had copies of any report you've made long before trial. If, during direct examination, your attorney asks a question and you can't remember what your notes reflect on that subject, rest assured your failing memory will not ruin the day. Jurors and judges recognize that some cases are quite complex and a witness may have a thick file full of information related to the case. No one expects you to have a photographic memory. When a witness fails to recollect something, an attorney can "refresh memory" by using the witness's notes. The exchange often goes something like this:

YOUR ATTORNEY: In addition to the beer cans, did you notice anything else in the Smiths' vehicle shortly after the collision?

WITNESS: *I don't recall right now.*

YOUR ATTORNEY: Would it refresh your memory if you could review your notes from February 13?

WITNESS: *Yes, it would.*

YOUR ATTORNEY: Your Honor, may I approach the witness for purposes of refreshing recollection?

JUDGE: *Yes, you may.*
(Attorney allows witness to read notes.)

YOUR ATTORNEY: Does that refresh your memory regarding what you saw?

WITNESS: *Yes it does. I also saw a cardboard box that said Budweiser on the side, the kind used to hold a twelve-pack of beer.*

Any good trial attorney will know well in advance of trial what you will say in response to any question posed. If you are not forthcoming with the anticipated answer, the attorney will find a way to bring it out.

Witnesses fear not looking intelligent when being cross-examined. Many of them think the jury won't believe them if they can't remember every detail about the case. This simply is not true.

Often, the wisest words in a witness's vocabulary are "I don't know." We all forget details. That's why we make reports.

If opposing counsel wants to score a point by using something you've included in one of your reports, the attorney will ask you directly about it. If you can't recall the details, the cross-examiner will use the same technique to refresh your recollection.

There are at least two reasons not to take notes to the witness stand. First, unless you know exactly where the information can be found in the papers on your lap, it will take some time to hunt it down. This can be distracting to the jury. Worse, if you fumble for too long, you may look inept. Anything that delays the trial is viewed with disfavor by the participants, including the judge and jury.

Second, there is a court rule[8] that says the cross-examiner may review any notes or papers you take with you to the stand. Let's assume you have some notes with you on the stand which, for one reason or another, were never provided to opposing counsel during the discovery process. If you take them with you to the witness stand, and they are revealed for the first time to the cross-examining attorney, you may be subjected to some nasty questions that imply you are hiding evidence to prejudice the case.

If your notes take up more than a page or two, opposing counsel may ask the judge for a recess in order to review them before continuing with your cross-examination. If the judge is so inclined, and this is more likely when the timing of the request coincides with the usual morning, noon, or afternoon breaks in the trial, a recess will be granted. You do not want this to happen. It gives opposing counsel more time to develop ammunition to discredit your testimony. In effect, you become your own worst enemy. Now opposing counsel can use the recess to pore over your notes looking for something that can be used to attack your credibility. Don't give opposing counsel this opportunity.

You may be asked to name the documents you have reviewed in preparation for your testimony that day. Always be truthful when responding. It is natural and expected that you will have reviewed your report before taking the stand.

It frequently happens that you have been subpoenaed to court at 9:00 a.m. but do not actually testify until late morning or early afternoon. You sit on a bench outside the courtroom passing the time. If opposing counsel sees you reading some material as you wait to testify, don't be surprised if you are asked to name the publication when you are on the stand. ■

TIP 22

Admit to talking to your attorney

An old but still fairly common tactic is for the cross-examiner to imply that your testimony has been staged. The jury should not believe you, the cross-examiner argues, because you are simply the opposition's puppet. The easiest way to counter this tactic is to discuss it with your attorney in advance. Your discussion might go like this:

> **WITNESS:** *I've heard that some attorneys will challenge a witness's credibility by implying that they've been told what to say at a pre-trial meeting. You and I know that isn't true. I assume you want me to be completely honest on the witness stand.*

> **YOUR ATTORNEY:** Of course.

> Then, when the issue is brought up at trial, the testimony might go this way:

OPPOSING COUNSEL: Your answers to your attorney's questions were so fluent. Tell me, Mr. Grayson, did you meet with Attorney Fox about this case?

WITNESS: *Yes, I did.*

OPPOSING COUNSEL: In fact, you've met with him more than once?

WITNESS: *Yes.*

OPPOSING COUNSEL: And he told you what questions he was going to ask you, didn't he?

WITNESS: *We discussed my testimony, yes.*

OPPOSING COUNSEL: (Smiles knowingly to the jury.) And your testimony went just as you planned, didn't it?

WITNESS: *I wouldn't put it quite that way.*

OPPOSING COUNSEL: No further questions.

JUDGE: *Any redirect? (that is, re-examination by the attorney who conducted direct examination)*

YOUR ATTORNEY: Yes, just a few, Your Honor. Mr. Grayson, it's true that we discussed, in general terms, what your testimony would be about today?

WITNESS: *Yes.*

YOUR ATTORNEY: We even discussed the tactic just used by opposing counsel, didn't we — how he might imply that your testimony was scripted?

WITNESS: *Yes, we did.*

YOUR ATTORNEY: What did we agree upon with regard to that tactic?

WITNESS: *We agreed that if I simply stuck to the truth, that was the best possible way to deal with it, and that's exactly what I've done.*

YOUR ATTORNEY: Thank you. Nothing further. ■

TIP 23

Do not interrupt the questioner

If you interrupt your attorney on direct examination, it usually happens because you have anticipated the question and are anxious to make your response. Strictly speaking, this violates court procedures, though it is unlikely anyone will object. But to interrupt is discourteous and implies your answer has been overly rehearsed — so never interrupt your attorney.

Don't interrupt opposing counsel either. Most witnesses interrupt opposing counsel because they disagree with the point being made through the attorney's question. When you answer before the full question is stated, opposing counsel may object or tell you, "Please let me finish my question before you respond." This makes you look argumentative as well as impolite. If you repeatedly interrupt, you may draw an admonition from the judge, something you always want to avoid.

Allow your attorney time to raise an objection to the question, rather than interrupting questions from opposing counsel. Far more often than you might expect, questions will be asked by attorneys that violate one of a host of legal rules. The rules of evidence guide all trials (each state devises its own set of rules, usually similar to the Federal Rules of Evidence), whether before a judge or jury. When opposing counsel asks a question in violation of one of the rules, your attorney may — but is not required to — object to the question. Timing is crucial! If you answer the question before your attorney objects, the damage cannot be undone.

If you have blurted out your answer and your attorney objects to the question, the judge may sustain your attorney's objection and say: "Members of the jury, you will disregard the answer to that last question." This doesn't help your case much and may actually reinforce the opposing position. So wait for opposing counsel to finish every question, and pause long enough for your attorney to object. Then, if there is no objection, answer the question. ■

TIP 24

Listen to the objections

You are not a attorney, and no one expects you to be one while you are on the witness stand. No one thinks you should have a command of the Federal Rules of Evidence when you formulate your answers to attorneys' questions. Nevertheless, it may be helpful for you to know something about some of the most common objections made during the course of any trial: hearsay, lack of foundation and speculation.

Hearsay

Perhaps the most frequent objection in any trial is hearsay, as in "Objection, Your Honor, the question calls for hearsay." Hearsay statements are out-of-court statements that are introduced for the purpose of proving the truth of the matter asserted in the statement. For example: "My daughter Linda said that Boyd gave her the black eye." Or: "My son told me he was roughed up at school by the Johnson boy." There can even be hearsay upon hearsay, or *double hearsay*, like: "The neighbor told my husband who told me it was her dog that bit the child."

If these statements are offered to prove the truth of the matter asserted (that Boyd hit Linda or that the Johnson boy roughed up the witness's son), they are hearsay. Generally speaking, hearsay is inadmissible in court. The reason for the hearsay rule goes to the very heart of our adversarial system of justice.

It is assumed that if both sides are able to present their case to the finder-of-fact, the truth will be brought out. This assumption rests on the guarantee of cross-examination. The theory is that truth will best be revealed if all witnesses are subject to close questioning by the opposition. The process of cross-examination should reveal weaknesses, gaps and inconsistencies in the testimony.

When hearsay is accepted into evidence, the party against whom the testimony is offered is cheated out of the opportunity of cross-examination. In the first example, without Linda on the witness stand, the opposing party cannot determine why she told her mother that Boyd struck her, or *if* she even told her mother such a thing.

But there are more than twenty well-recognized exceptions to the hearsay rule. The most common is the exception for statements made by an opposing party. If Boyd told Linda he was going to keep punching her until she started listening to him, his statement could be brought out at trial through Linda's testimony, because it is an admission by the opposing party.

When opposing counsel objects to a question from your attorney on the basis of hearsay, the objection will require the judge to mentally review the exceptions to the general rule and decide whether or not you can answer. Wait for the ruling before answering. If the judge *sustains* (upholds) the objection made by opposing counsel, your attorney will rephrase the question or move to another topic.

Frequently, the question may not ask for hearsay, but the witness's response will include it nonetheless. For example:

YOUR ATTORNEY: Do you know how Linda got her black eye?

WITNESS: *Well, she told me that Boyd hit her with his fist.*

Opposing counsel will properly object that the response includes hearsay and should be stricken from the record. Most likely, the judge will agree.

A correct response to the question would be "Not directly, no," or "I only know what Linda told me." Attorneys seek to avoid objectionable questions, so *listen carefully to the exact words used.* Avoid giving an answer that includes hearsay unless you've discussed the matter with your attorney. By understanding the rationale behind this common objection, your responses are less likely to be stricken from the record.

Lack of Foundation

Another frequent objection is that a question *lacks foundation.* As with other objections, if the judge agrees, you will not be allowed to answer the question even though you clearly know the answer!

Assume you were involved in a traffic accident and you believe the other driver was driving under the influence of intoxicating beverages. Your attorney has asked you questions about your name, occupation, and the events leading to your confrontation with the other motorist. These questions follow:

YOUR ATTORNEY: When you first saw Mr. Schmidt after the collision, where was he?

WITNESS: *He was standing by his car.*

YOUR ATTORNEY: Do you have an opinion as to whether or not Mr. Schmidt was under the influence of intoxicating liquor that night?

OPPOSING COUNSEL: *Objection! Lack of foundation.*

JUDGE: Sustained.

The objection was sustained because your attorney had not laid the necessary groundwork, the foundation, for asking you the ultimate question. To lay the groundwork, your attorney would have to ask you several questions about Mr. Schmidt's conduct and your observations. What was it about the way he walked, talked, smelled, and looked that gave you the impression he was under the influence? In addition, your attorney would want to question you specifically about your experience with people who have consumed alcohol. Once that is done, you would be allowed to give your opinion about Mr. Schmidt's degree of impairment.

Understanding the lack of foundation will give you a better understanding of where the attorney is going with the questions.

Speculation

A third common objection is that the question calls for *speculation.* For example:

PLAINTIFF'S ATTORNEY:	Ms. Okai, where were you when you heard the crashing sound?
WITNESS:	*I was in bed upstairs.*
PLAINTIFF'S ATTORNEY:	Did you smell anything?
WITNESS:	*Not right away, but later I did smell smoke, as if something was burning.*
PLAINTIFF'S ATTORNEY:	What did you think happened?
DEFENDANT'S ATTORNEY:	*Objection, Your Honor. The question calls for speculation.*
JUDGE:	Sustained.

The basis for the objection is that the witness has not shown enough knowledge to answer the question and would be speculating, or guessing, in order to give a response.

This objection is also frequently made when a witness begins an answer with the words, "I guess," "I think," or "I believe." These are red flags to opposing counsel. Do not use them. It is important to say only what you *know*. If you don't know the answer, don't pretend that you do or speculate. If you do know the answer, be forthright and confident in your response. ■

TIP 25

Do not converse with opposing counsel

If you don't say anything, you won't be called upon to repeat it.

—Calvin Coolidge

After you have testified, especially if your testimony was lengthy, the judge may call a recess. Many attorneys for the opposition use this opportunity to obtain information from the witness who has just left the stand. "So what?" you think to yourself, "I'm done testifying. There can't be any harm in talking to the opposition now."

There are several reasons for avoiding opposing counsel. First, whether you want to or not, you may be recalled to testify by either side in the case. Your attorney may want you to clarify some testimony or counteract something another witness said. Once you resume the stand, you are subject to cross-examination. Although the cross-examining attorney is supposed to confine the questions to the subject matter just covered by your attorney, judges are sometimes very lenient in allowing cross-examination on incidental matters.

Opposing counsel may believe you have information valuable to her client that was not brought out when you were last on the witness stand; she then can call you as her witness. Some seemingly small detail you gave her in the hallway may be magnified in the courtroom and turn the whole case around. If you inadvertently give opposing counsel some valuable information, it will be used to hurt your testimony.

Even if opposing counsel doesn't get any information of value from you, the very fact that you were seen having the conversation may be helpful to the other side. If any juror sees you conversing with opposing counsel, maybe laughing at a joke together, looking like chums, that juror may assume you don't think the case is a serious one. Why else would you so readily "consort with the enemy?" While you know this is not reality, the juror does not.

When approached by opposing counsel, politely, but firmly, say that you are not free to discuss the case unless your attorney is present. Attorneys can be very charming; they may only want to take a moment of your time to "clarify" something. Or they may be cantankerous. Stick to your guns, no matter how persuasive or threatening opposing counsel becomes. If opposing counsel warns, "You can talk to me now, or I can subpoena you and make you return to court," you should respond, "Do whatever you think you must," then walk away.

Apply this same caution to anyone associated with opposing counsel. It may be a legal assistant or a witness sympathetic to the opposition who attempts to get information from you. Regardless of who approaches you from the opponent's camp, do not engage in conversation about anything related to the case unless your attorney has approved it in advance.

This is good advice even after the jury retires to deliberate on a verdict. There is always the possibility of a mistrial or a new trial following an appeal. Assume you may have to testify about this matter again. ■

How to Be Verbally Persuasive on the Witness Stand

The next several tips will keep judge and jury aligned with you and willing to give credence to what you have to say.

TIP 26

Tell the truth

A liar needs a good memory.

—Quintilian

There are many reasons to always tell the truth on the witness stand; not the least of these is the oath you have taken. Whether you "swear to tell the truth, the whole truth, and nothing but the truth, so help you God," or "affirm under the penalties of perjury to tell the truth," you are legally bound to answer questions truthfully. If you lie, you can be charged with perjury, which is a felony in most states.

In reality, very few people are charged with perjury. Defense attorneys in criminal cases rarely have their clients take the witness stand. Attorneys have an ethical obligation not to present testimony believed to be false. If the client tells the attorney that he intends to testify falsely, the attorney cannot call the client to the stand without violating the Code of Professional Responsibility, the ethical rules governing attorneys' conduct.

Even when defendants do testify and a jury disbelieves them, as shown by a guilty verdict, it is extremely rare that the local prosecutor pursues perjury charges. The reasons are practical. First, to prove perjury there must be evidence of a false statement under oath. This is not so simple to prove. If a witness's statement is in any way based on perception or opinion, it is almost impossible to prove intentional lying.

Secondly, it is not enough to prove a misstatement under oath. The misstatement must relate to an issue which is "material" to the general matter testified about. For example, in a slip-and-fall case, if the plaintiff testified he slipped on the defendant's icy sidewalk when, in fact, he had slipped on someone else's property, that is a material matter and the plaintiff could be charged with perjury. But if the plaintiff testified the sidewalk was completely covered in ice while knowing that it was only partially covered, the false testimony would likely be deemed immaterial.

However, you should be honest about even those matters that do not go to the heart of the case. You're much better off being completely candid, even when it hurts.

In virtually every case which goes to trial, there are weaknesses on both sides. The adversarial system is designed to reveal these weaknesses to the finder-of-fact. Just as there are weaknesses in each party's case, there are usually weaknesses in the testimony of each witness. Often, there are facts known by each witness that bolster the other side's case.

The temptation is to cover them up or lie about them. Aside from the immoral and illegal aspects of lying on the witness stand, it is usually a poor strategy because any competent attorney may learn of them in advance of trial and bring them out. An attempt to hide unfavorable evidence usually backfires. Opposing counsel will go to great lengths to discredit the witness who has attempted to keep it from coming to light.

Rational jurors do not expect cases to be airtight. They know that nothing is all black or white. They expect certain inconsistencies and contradictions. But they also expect complete honesty from everyone testifying (with the possible exception of the defendant in a criminal case). They expect you to admit unfavorable facts if you have personal knowledge of them. When you candidly admit them, you enhance your credibility with jurors and the judge.

Good attorneys use testimonial inconsistencies to their advantage. They will argue that the inconsistencies show that the witness is untrustworthy *in all respects*. Opposing counsel will counter that the jury should believe the witness who admitted even unfavorable facts.

Don't hide mistakes. The lab scientist who admits misplacing a piece of evidence, the social worker who admits a bias about a particularly obnoxious family member, or the secretary who frankly admits failing to send a letter on a particular day — they all come across as more credible because they freely admitted their errors.

Defensiveness has just the opposite effect and gives opposing counsel something to focus on in an attempt to divert attention from a client's guilt or negligence. A case that was a hopeless loser for the other side takes on new life; now it is all about the "lying witness." Don't let it happen to you. Tell the truth, always. ■

TIP 27

Avoid humor

A joke, even if it be a lame one, is nowhere so keenly
relished or quickly applauded as in a murder trial.

—Mark Twain

Because trials are often emotionally charged events, tensions run high in the courtroom. To ease the tension, sometimes injecting a clever comment or joke seems appropriate. Refrain from it.

Not everyone has a sense of humor. A corollary is that we all have different ideas about what is funny and what is not. The odds are that someone on the jury will think your attempt at humor is about as funny as a trip to the mortuary. You may not lose points with every juror for being quick-witted, but you may well offend some.

A defense attorney may want to inject humor in the case. The rationale is that the jury is more likely to acquit the defendant or return a smaller money judgment against him if jurors believe the case isn't very serious. For that reason, prosecutors and plaintiffs' attorneys seldom want humor in the courtroom during trial. By engaging in humor, you may be playing into the hands of the defendant.

One final reason not to use humor on the witness stand is that it seldom translates well into print. Remember that an appellate court, reviewing a transcript of the trial will not have the benefit of everything seen and heard in the courtroom. They will have only the cold, hard record. The comical look on someone's face and the tone of the words spoken may make something seem downright hilarious in court that will fail to come across as even slightly humorous on paper. ■

TIP 28

Keep calm

Jurors love someone who can maintain composure while undergoing tough cross-examination. They've watched enough television and movies to know that attorneys are given plenty of latitude when cross-examining a witness. Many of them expect the cross-examiner to be ruthless and crass because that is the style they've seen in the media.

The truth is, far too many cross-examiners are not as well prepared as the actors on the screen. Their questions tend to be undramatic. Cross-examination, in the real world, often tends to be overly long and not particularly productive.

The best cross-examiners are concise and unemotional. They cut and run, often scoring points that do not become obvious until later in the trial. Irving Younger, one of the best trial attorneys, taught students to never attempt to make more than three points during cross-examination. "Get in, slice and dice, and get out."

Nevertheless, there is at least a decent chance that you will run across an attorney who confuses rudeness with good trial advocacy. Although you may have to grit your teeth, remain professional and low key at all times. Respond to sarcasm without a tinge of it in your voice. Respond to phony anger with tranquility. I suggest occasionally using "Sir" or "Ma'am" in your answers: "No, sir, I would have to disagree with that" or "Yes, ma'am, that is how I conducted the test."

Jurors don't like hotheads, and they don't trust people who lose control on the witness stand, though they seldom hold it against a repugnant attorney who engages in rude behavior. The Canons of Ethics for attorneys require them to "zealously represent" their clients. Perhaps jurors know — at some deep level — that attorneys are required to fight hard and even get "dirty," so jurors forgive them their excesses. "He's just doing his job." But they may discount *your* testimony, if you lose your composure on the stand. It's a double standard and hardly a fair one, but it is reality.

Keeping your cool on the witness stand is generally good advice. However, it seems that when it comes to human behavior, for every rule there is an exception. There are times when the jury or judge not only accepts emotionalism from a witness, but expects it.

In domestic violence cases, jurors are often surprised when a victim does not show anger on the witness stand. They are even more perplexed when the victim does not come to the trial or recants earlier testimony, attempting to exonerate the perpetrator of any guilt. "Why does she protect him?" and "Why doesn't she just leave him?" are questions frequently on the minds of jurors.

Research shows that victims of battering spouses are at **greater** risk of serious injury or death immediately after leaving, than if they stay. Domestic violence is invariably about control. When the abuser loses control over the victim — when she leaves — the abuser will often go to any lengths to regain that control, or sometimes kill her if he can't. Coupled with the financial insecurity of most victims and a host of familial or religious pressures, it is unsurprising that victims stay in the same home with their abusers.

If the victim testifies against the abuser and shows legitimate anger toward him, she may help gain his conviction but lose financial support and a caretaker for the children. If the victim testifies and does not show any emotion, jurors may wonder about her lack of response. "Why isn't she more upset about this?" The victim is caught on the horns of a dilemma.

One of the most bizarre cases I ever presided over as a judge involved a mom, Elizabeth, who testified about the sexual abuse of her daughter, Kate. Elizabeth was married to Larry — but he was not the father of Kate, then 15 years old. Larry was a truck driver and a coarse man who had previously been convicted of child sexual abuse with his own daughter. He spent time in jail on that charge, and his first wife divorced him.

Larry ruled the household with an iron fist. Both Elizabeth and Kate were overweight, so Larry insisted they do calisthenics every day and jog around the house whenever he so commanded. To gain compliance with his orders, he tortured a family pet and threatened to bring in his "buddies in the black helicopters," who would do the same to Elizabeth and Kate.

One summer, Kate complained to Elizabeth about menstrual cramps. Elizabeth shared this information with Larry, who promptly said he was trained in such matters and could easily diagnose the problem. He would do so using what he called a "penile probe." Kate turned him down repeatedly, but he was adamant. Kate asked her mother about it, and Elizabeth told her to do whatever she thought best. Finally, Kate caved in to Larry's constant pressure.

So one day, Kate and Larry got into bed together. Kate was wearing pajamas while Larry was nude. Under the bed sheet, he took off her pajama bottoms and conducted his penile probe. Incredibly, Elizabeth sat on the corner of the bed holding Kate's hand during the "procedure." Afterwards, Larry opined there was nothing wrong with Kate; she was just fat.

As I heard this testimony unfolding, I did my best to mask my revulsion and disgust. I wholeheartedly believe the jury was doing the same thing. As Elizabeth related the events, she showed almost no emotion. Kate was no different and scarcely looked at Larry seated next to his attorney. For his part, Larry denied everything; there was no forensic evidence to prove the rape. Under the rules, the prosecution could not tell the jury about Larry's earlier conviction for child sexual abuse.

The jurors deliberated longer than I thought they would, but eventually found Larry guilty of rape. I spoke with the jurors after they delivered their verdict. They were upset not only with Larry but equally — if not more so — with Elizabeth. The jurors demanded to know if Elizabeth had been charged with any crime. If she hadn't, they wanted to know how they could influence the prosecutor to bring criminal charges against her.

In retrospect, I'm not sure Elizabeth had the mental makeup to do much other than what she did. Her lack of emotion on the witness stand was consistent with her downtrodden, subservient role. She could no more show anger at Larry while testifying than she could stand up to him when he made his horrible suggestion in the first place.

The point of this is to emphasize that there are times when judges and juries expect a witness to be something other than "cool, calm and collected." Under the bizarre circumstances of Larry's trial, an angry outburst by Elizabeth or Kate would not have been condemned. It may even have made their testimony more credible.

Each case is unique. Jurors, I think, expect witnesses to react emotionally to events that caused serious psychological or physical trauma. But — on the other hand — showing hostility or coming unhinged on the stand over a small property damage claim might very well alienate the jury. ■

TIP 29

Choose your words carefully and use powerful language

The difference between the right word and the almost right word is the difference between lightning and the lightning bug.

—Mark Twain

Psychologists have demonstrated that how words are used in asking a question affects the answer. Test subjects in a virtual environment witnessed a car collision. They were then asked a series of questions. One group of test subjects was asked, "How far from the street were you when you saw the red car?" Another group was asked, "How close to the street were you when you saw the red car?" Those who answered the first question gave an approximation significantly longer in distance than those who answered the second question. Savvy attorneys are aware of this and may incorporate the appropriate term — from their perspective — in their question to you. Listen for it.

Seasoned trial attorneys also know that jurors look at the attorney and client as one entity. To take advantage of this concept, attorneys will cozy up to an unsavory client in public to give jurors the impression that they are friends. The implicit argument is, "Look, folks, this guy can't be too bad because I'm a college-educated professional and he's a buddy of mine."

Opposing attorneys will often personalize the client by calling him "Bob" rather than "Mr. Fleischer." Conversely, the same attorney will attempt to depersonalize others by referring to them as the plaintiff, the petitioner, the alleged victim, or the respondent. The attorney might refer to opponents by their profession: the chiropractor or the accountant. This is an attempt to create a greater psychological distance between the jury and that person.

You too can influence jurors' perception through your choice of language. Different words permit the listener to draw subtle distinctions. You can refer to a person you want the jury to view favorably by his or her first name.

Description of events and environments can be bland or intricate. A night can be "dark" or "so black I could not see my hand in front of my face." You could say an inebriated person "walked" down the sidewalk. But you could use strong verbs like wove, shuffled, stumbled, lurched, or crept.

If you want to emphasize the seriousness of an injury, you can say laceration rather than cut, or contusion, rather than bruise. You can refer to a car crash as an accident or a collision. Collision implies fault; accident implies the incident could not have been prevented.

Just as you can convey confidence and professionalism through your nonverbal language, you can enhance your credibility through the use of powerful language. To be powerful, the words you use must not be ambiguous, and your phrasing should be positive.

The opposite of powerful language is weak or unconvincing language. Examples of weak language include any sentence which begins: "It seems like" or "I believe." A witness who describes a scene as "kind of like" signals to the jury that some confusion exists in the witness's mind about the event. When you are stating an opinion, you need not preface it with, "In my opinion . . ." The jury knows it is your opinion. Be positive. Be clear. You will persuade.

The words you choose influence the listener, and the choice is entirely yours. You can paint the picture the way you like, while not straying from the truth. A thesaurus is a useful tool for the well-prepared witness. ■

TIP 30

Use examples, stories and analogies

You never truly understand a thing until you can explain it to your grandmother.

—Albert Einstein

Psychologists report that jurors remember analogies, stories and examples better than any other testimony. This is especially true when complicated matters are explained to those who have little or no background in the subject area.

In a murder case, the defendant pled not guilty by reason of insanity. A psychiatrist was called upon to testify about the defendant's mental health. The defense had made quite a production out of showing the defendant had suffered a concussion on the night of the murder. The psychiatrist explained to the jury that simply because the defendant suffered a concussion did not mean that he was more prone to mental illness or defect than anyone else.

The jury consisted of older-than-average citizens, and the psychiatrist used an apt analogy. "Experiencing a concussion," he said, "is like the switchboard operator in an old-time telephone office. All of the phone wires are jerked out of their sockets and all activity stops. But the phone equipment is not really damaged. Plug the wires back in and the connections are fine. People can talk to one another again. The brain operates in the same way. The concussion knocked out all the connections for a while, but when the patient regained consciousness, most likely there was no long-term damage. The individual could have been back to normal almost immediately."

Examples and analogies work best when they arise from our shared experiences. Our culture is changing, some say dramatically, in that those shared experiences are now more often associated with the visual media. References to literary characters or novels may draw blank stares from many younger jurors. Instead, television sitcom characters or movie roles may be better known.

Since you will usually not know the makeup of the jury until the day you testify, it helps to give this matter some forethought. How will you explain something to the grandmother in the second row of the jury box while also clarifying it for the nineteen-year-old in the front row? What example can you use that will be equally clear to both? With preparation, you will find something that works for everyone. ■

TIP 31

Avoid using overstatement and understatement

Considerable research has been done on the kind of language that is most persuasive to others. Researchers found that the use of intensifiers — words such as very, certainly, and definitely — weakens the credibility of the speaker. To the speaker they seem to increase the force of a statement. But they have the opposite effect on the listener, who senses that the speaker lacks confidence in the accuracy of the statement. Other intensifiers are so, too, quite, extremely, really, and definitely.

Another form of weak language is the hedge. Phrases like sort of, kind of, maybe, probably, and I think convey to the listener that the assertion of the witness lacks certainty. Hedges and intensifiers, should be avoided when testifying.[9] Keep your statements simple and straightforward. ■

TIP 32

Pay attention to cadence and inflection

Too often, I have watched as expert witnesses literally put jurors to sleep. It wasn't that they didn't know their subject matter. On the contrary, they were intelligent and experienced. The problem was their delivery.

The next time you watch a national news program, pay attention to the voices of the news anchor and reporters. Better yet, turn away from the television screen and just listen. Almost invariably, these professionals are able to keep your attention by the tone, inflection, and cadence of their speech.

While there is little you can do to change the overall tone of your voice without the help of a speech pathologist, you can work on your inflection and cadence. Inflection is simply the emphasis you give your words, and cadence is the speed at which you speak them. The sure way to bore your audience is to speak in a monotone. The trick of the news professionals is to use *variety*.

A good reader uses varied inflection and cadence to make a children's story more enjoyable. While you will not exaggerate your presentation to this degree, a more subtle use of inflection in your voice will make your testimony more appealing.

If you are serious about improving your presentation skills, join an organization like Storytelling Foundation International (www.storytellingcenter.com) and learn from the real professionals. You don't have to be an actor or actress to better convey your message to juries. ■

CHAPTER THREE

How to Survive Direct and Cross-Examination

What to Expect During Direct Examination

A witness in court or in a deposition is questioned by *direct examination* or cross-examination. Generally speaking, direct examination is conducted by the attorney who calls the witness to the stand. Cross-examination is conducted by the opposing attorney. There are specific rules which govern direct examination.

An attorney's style of questioning on direct examination parallels a journalist's. They ask the five Ws: "who, what, where, when, and why." A brief example of direct examination follows:

ATTORNEY: Please state your name.

WITNESS: My name is Robin Edwards.

ATTORNEY: What is your occupation?

WITNESS: I am a sales manager for Dan's Friendly Automart.

ATTORNEY: Were you working on the evening of July 1 of this year?

WITNESS: Yes, I was.

ATTORNEY: Tell us where you were around 6:30 that evening.

WITNESS: I was in the car lot at the corner of 7th Avenue and Oak Street.

ATTORNEY: Did you notice anything unusual at that time?

WITNESS: Yes. I saw an accident where a black SUV ran into the back end of a green minivan.

ATTORNEY: What happened next?

> **WITNESS:** *I saw a man stumbling as he got out of the minivan. He appeared to have blood on his shirt and face.*
>
> **ATTORNEY:** What did you do then?

The cardinal rule for attorneys conducting direct examination is to let the witness fill in the answers to who, what, when, where, and why questions without giving any suggestions. These questions are called *non-leading*; they do not lead the witness to the preferred answer.

The rules of evidence apply at most court proceedings and at all trials. These rules specify that the attorney conducting direct examination must use non-leading questions.

If the attorney violates the rule by asking a leading question, opposing counsel may object to the form of the question; the judge will likely *sustain* the objection and order the question to be rephrased. Here is an example:

> **ATTORNEY:** Where were you around 6:30 that evening?
>
> **WITNESS:** *I was in the car lot at the corner of 7th Avenue and Oak Street.*
>
> **ATTORNEY:** Did you notice anything unusual at that time on the street nearby?
>
> **WITNESS:** *Yes, I did. I saw a car accident.*
>
> **ATTORNEY:** Did you see a man stumbling out of a minivan, bleeding from the head?
>
> **OPPOSING COUNSEL:** *Objection, Your Honor. Counsel is leading the witness.*
>
> **JUDGE:** Sustained. Please rephrase your question, counsel.
>
> **ATTORNEY:** *What did you see immediately after the vehicles collided?*

Note that opposing counsel could also have objected to the question, "Did you notice anything unusual at that time on the street nearby?" because that question is also leading. However, most courts routinely allow leading questions when they relate to preliminary matters. Attorneys realize this and probably would not object to the question.

In short, during direct examination, the finder-of-fact hears testimony from the witness in his or her own words. During cross-examination, the judge or jury hears a different kind of testimony. This testimony is typically an affirmation of events as worded by the interrogating attorney.

What to Expect During Cross-Examination

Cross-examination is at the very heart of the adversarial system. Its basic purpose is to raise doubts about the accuracy of your testimony. In training, attorneys are repeatedly warned never to ask a question on cross-examination to which they do not know the answer with certainty. Attorneys learn, often the hard way, not to go on fishing expeditions, particularly with witnesses who are hostile. Here is a sample cross-examination where the defense attorney in a criminal case decided to go fishing:

DEFENSE: Officer, did you see my client fleeing the scene?

OFFICER: No, sir, but I subsequently observed a person matching the description of the offender running several blocks away.

DEFENSE: Who provided you this description?

OFFICER: The officer who responded to the scene.

DEFENSE: A fellow officer provided the description of this so-called offender. Do you trust your fellow officers?

OFFICER: Yes, sir, with my life.

DEFENSE: With your life. Then let me ask you this, officer, do you have a locker room in the police station, a room where you change your clothes in preparation for your daily duties?

OFFICER: Yes, sir, we do.

DEFENSE: And do you have a locker in that room?

OFFICER: Yes, sir, I do.

DEFENSE: And do you have a lock on your locker?

OFFICER: Yes, sir.

DEFENSE: Now why is it, officer, if you trust your fellow officers with your life, that you find it necessary to lock your locker in a room you share with those same officers?

OFFICER: You see, sir, we share the building with a court complex, and sometimes attorneys have been known to walk through that room.

(With that, the courtroom erupted in laughter and a recess was promptly called.)

In a typical cross-examination, questions are designed to confirm the information contained in the query. "Isn't it true that you drive a blue, four-door, Honda Accord?" Not only does the leading question put into the record information phrased exactly as desired, the technique has the additional benefit of allowing the questioner to control the witness. In most cases, questions are framed so that the only appropriate answer is "yes" or "no." While a witness is never bound to answer in this fashion, it is usually appropriate to do so.

Questions about observable activities almost always must be answered "yes" or "no." But often the focal issue in the case revolves around intent or some other state of mind. The attorney may try to hem in the witness with questions about conduct, gaining concession after concession. Then the attorney moves to seek an admission of what was in the witness's mind at the time. A vigilant witness can, and often should, refuse to answer "yes" or "no" if that would not be a truthful answer.

For example, assume you are a parent in a child custody dispute. Opposing counsel is attempting to show you love your children less than your spouse does.

OPPOSING COUNSEL: Isn't it true, Mr. Graff, you have seen your children only twice in the past month?

WITNESS: *Yes.*

OPPOSING COUNSEL: And in that same time period you called them only one time?

WITNESS: *Yes.*

OPPOSING COUNSEL: You didn't write them any letters, did you?

WITNESS: *Ever, or just in the last month?*

OPPOSING COUNSEL: In the last month.

WITNESS: *No, I didn't.*

OPPOSING COUNSEL: And you didn't send them any cards?

WITNESS: *No.*

OPPOSING COUNSEL: No emails, either?

WITNESS: *No.*

OPPOSING COUNSEL: Visitation with your kids isn't very important to you, is it?

WITNESS: *Yes, it is.*

OPPOSING COUNSEL: But you didn't do all that you could to spend more time with your children, did you?

WITNESS: *It's been a particularly hectic month. Let me explain . . .*

OPPOSING COUNSEL: (interrupting) Just answer the question, yes or no.

WITNESS: *It's not that simple. I . . .*

OPPOSING COUNSEL: (interrupting again) Your Honor, I ask that you instruct the witness to answer my question. It's a simple yes or no question.

JUDGE: *Can you answer the question "yes" or "no?"*

WITNESS: *No, I can't honestly do that, Your Honor.*

JUDGE: Then, answer the question as truthfully as you can.

In the alternative, the judge might ask opposing counsel to rephrase the question. The point is, you do not necessarily have to answer the question in the manner expected if that would require you to violate your oath to tell the truth. But if the judge instructs you to answer yes or no, follow that order. Have faith that your attorney, on *redirect* examination, will let you give the extra details you wanted to explain earlier.

The rules of evidence limit the cross-examiner to questioning you about only those subjects touched on during direct examination. But the rule is not rigidly followed. For example, cross-examiners are generally given considerable latitude in attacking the credibility of the witness. It is fair game for the cross-examiner to question your memory or perception.

Even when the cross-examiner strays far from the subjects covered on direct examination, a judge may allow it despite an objection. The cross-examiner responds: "Yes, Your Honor, I know that I've exceeded the scope of direct examination, but I ask for some latitude. Otherwise, I will subpoena Mr. Olson as our witness and make him sit here for several hours (or days) until I call him to the stand. I would rather finish with him so that he might be on his way." Especially in bench trials, a judge will usually allow the cross-examiner to proceed.

If you were called upon to give an opinion during direct examination, prepare to have the basis of that opinion severely challenged. The challenge may come in several ways. First, the cross-examiner may question your expertise. This can be done by asking questions critical of your education or experience. Secondly, the cross-examiner may ask questions designed to show that you did not have all of the facts at your disposal when you arrived at your opinion, or that you based your opinion on facts assumed to be true which, in fact, were not.

In many parts of the country, court rules provide that attorneys do the bulk of their questioning from the counsel table. In these jurisdictions, attorneys must ask permission from the judge before coming up to the witness stand to ask a question. Judges routinely grant the request "to approach the witness" so long as there is a legitimate reason for doing so, like showing the witness an exhibit.

Where the rules are not restrictive, the seated attorney may pepper the witness with questions. When the witness does not give the answers the attorney wants to hear, he or she may stand up, give the witness a scowl, and walk toward the stand, asking a confrontational question en route. A belligerent tone of voice, together with imposing physical presence, can cause a witness to waver. Women seem to be victims of this bullying tactic more often than men.

If an objection is made by opposing counsel ("Objection, Your Honor, counsel is badgering the witness"), the judge may intervene and order the attorney back to his seat. The best way to guard against such intimidation is to be aware of the tactic beforehand. Then you can respond more slowly than usual, without sarcasm or anger, but firmly. Disagree without being disagreeable. You are not trying to convince the attorney of anything. It is the jury and judge you need to impress with your demeanor.

How Attorneys Discredit a Witness

By asking leading or suggestive questions, an attorney can dictate the order in which subjects are taken up, as well as the pace of the cross-examination. A smart attorney may begin cross-examination by inquiring into relatively innocuous or non-controversial matters. He may have a friendly demeanor and give the impression that he and the witness are allies in a joint mission to seek the truth. This is *not* what the attorney really has in mind. Rather, these introductory questions are designed to curry favor with the jury and perhaps elicit information the witness might not otherwise volunteer.

But after the attorney has squeezed all of the favorable evidence from the witness in this non-confrontational manner, the gloves come off. Now the attorney, in order to zealously represent his client, must discredit the testimony of the witness. The process of discrediting testimony is called impeachment.

Trial advocacy expert Irving Younger described three common ways of impeaching a witness showing bias or prejudice, poor memory, or poor perception. In addition, opposing counsel may seek to discredit a witness by reviewing inconsistent statements, by attacking the witness's character, and by demonstrating that experts have a contrary view.

This jury instruction, a variation of which is given by most judges, sets out quite well the various avenues of attack an attorney might take in attempting to discredit or impeach a witness:

> Another part of your duties as jurors is to decide how credible or believable each witness was. This is your duty, not mine. It is up to you to decide if a witness's testimony was believable and how much weight you think it deserves. You are free to believe everything that a witness said, or only part of it, or none of it at all. But you should act reasonably and carefully in making these decisions.
>
> Let me suggest some things for you to consider in evaluating each witness's testimony.
>
> • Ask yourself if the witness was able to clearly see or hear the events. Sometimes even an honest witness may not have been able to see or hear what was happening, and may make a mistake.
>
> • Ask yourself how good the witness's memory seemed to be. Did the witness seem able to accurately remember what happened?
>
> • Ask yourself if there was anything else that may have interfered with the witness's ability to perceive or remember the events.
>
> • Ask yourself how the witness acted while testifying. Did the witness appear honest? Or did the witness appear to be lying?
>
> • Ask yourself if the witness had any relationship to any party in this case, or anything to gain or lose from the case, that might influence his testimony. Ask yourself if the witness had any bias or prejudice or reason for testifying that might cause him to lie or to slant the testimony in favor of one side or the other.

- Ask yourself if the witness testified inconsistently while on the witness stand, or if he said or did something or failed to say or do something at any other time that is inconsistent with what he said while testifying. If you believe that the witness was inconsistent, ask yourself if this makes his testimony less believable. Sometimes it may; other times it may not. Consider whether the inconsistency was about something important or about some unimportant detail. Ask yourself if it seemed like an innocent mistake or if it seemed deliberate.

- And ask yourself how believable the witness's testimony was in light of all the other evidence. Was it supported or contradicted by other evidence that you found believable? If you believe that a witness's testimony was contradicted by other evidence, remember that people sometimes forget things and that even two honest people who witness the same event may not describe it exactly the same way.

These are only some of the things that you may consider in deciding how believable each witness was. You may also consider other things that you think shed some light on the witness's credibility. Use your common sense and your everyday experience in dealing with other people. Then decide what testimony you believe and how much weight you think it deserves.

Impeachment by Demonstrating Prejudice or Bias

Prejudice means holding an opinion not based on proof or competent evidence. People typically refer to prejudice as an irrational opinion, usually negative in nature. But prejudice, which really means prejudging or judging before the fact, can be positive. For example, note the inclination of jurors to automatically believe the testimony of clergy.

Biases, too, can be negative or positive. While we all have biases, no one likes to admit them, and we are quick to condemn those people whose biases or prejudices are exposed. This is especially true on the witness stand. One of the most potent weapons of a skilled attorney is the ability to show how a witness's perception is biased.

Opposing counsel may expose a witness's educational background, training, or employment history to imply bias. If it can be shown that a witness is likely to sympathize with the other side because they do the same kind of work, it may impact the jury's view of the witness. Similarly, if the cross-examiner can show that someone has never held a steady job or has minimal training in the subject at issue, the witness's testimony may be impeached.

Some attorneys like to imply bias when a witness refuses to confer with them about the case in advance of trial. This does not mean you should meet with opposing counsel before testifying. You shouldn't, unless it is by way of a deposition, or it is done with the consent and in the presence of your attorney. An opposing attorney may, in a huff, inquire, "Isn't it true, Ms. Smith, that you refused to meet with me or even to talk to me about the case, when I made that request of you?" If it is true, a good response would be, "Not exactly, sir. I told you I would be happy to meet with you if my attorney was present, but you didn't seem interested in that."

Here is an example of a cross-examination intended to impeach the witness by showing bias or prejudice.

The scenario: a social worker testified on direct examination that Sarah Jones is the victim of child sexual abuse at the hands of her stepfather, John Jones.

ATTORNEY FOR JOHN JONES: You don't particularly like my client, do you?

SOCIAL WORKER: *I wouldn't necessarily say that.*

ATTORNEY: But the truth is you are not fond of Mr. Jones, wouldn't that be fair to say?

SOCIAL WORKER: *I suppose that's fair.*

ATTORNEY: Did you consult with anyone else in your office before you went over to interview Sarah Jones?

SOCIAL WORKER: *Yes, I consulted with another social worker, Ms. Gunderson.*

ATTORNEY: Ms. Gunderson had investigated a previous allegation involving my client, isn't that correct?

SOCIAL WORKER: *Yes, that's right.*

ATTORNEY: No action was taken against Mr. Jones as a result of that earlier investigation, was there?

SOCIAL WORKER: *None that I'm aware of.*

ATTORNEY: But Ms. Gunderson had tried to get custody of Sarah taken away from John, isn't that true?

SOCIAL WORKER: *It's true that a petition was filed to terminate his parental rights.*

ATTORNEY: In layman's terms, that means that John would have lost his daughter?

SOCIAL WORKER: *His step-daughter, that's right.*

ATTORNEY: So as far as you were concerned, John had gotten by once before, but this time would be different; that was your attitude when you went to interview Sarah?

SOCIAL WORKER: *No, I wouldn't agree with that.*

ATTORNEY: But you tended to believe Sarah was abused before you even talked to her, didn't you?

SOCIAL WORKER: *No, I had an open mind.*

ATTORNEY: The fact that the home had been investigated in the past had absolutely no impact on you at all?

SOCIAL WORKER: *I may have taken it into consideration after I conducted the interview and was making my recommendation.*

ATTORNEY: But you would have this jury believe that it didn't even enter your mind that John had been previously investigated when you went to interview Sarah?

SOCIAL WORKER: *It may have crossed my mind.*

ATTORNEY: The truth is you already had an impression of my client before you talked to Sarah.

SOCIAL WORKER: *Well, somewhat, but ...*

ATTORNEY: Yet you didn't excuse yourself so that someone objective could do that interview, did you?

SOCIAL WORKER: *No, I didn't think that was necessary.*

ATTORNEY: If you had asked for help because of a conflict of interest, such help was available, was it not?

SOCIAL WORKER: *I suppose so, although everyone is very busy.*

ATTORNEY: You could have insisted because you had an obvious conflict of interest.

SOCIAL WORKER: *It's not that simple.*

ATTORNEY: You knew the importance of that interview to my client; that his very freedom, not to mention his reputation, was on the line, didn't you?

SOCIAL WORKER: *I just try to do my job the best I can.*

ATTORNEY: You didn't even take along another professional to listen in on the interview, did you?

SOCIAL WORKER: *I didn't think that was necessary.*

ATTORNEY: And now my client stands unfairly accused because you failed to take some simple precautions. No further questions.

My advice to witnesses is to answer these questions unemotionally and without apparent resentment. Knowing they are coming will help a witness keep calm on the witness stand. To reduce the impact of these questions implying bias and prejudice, your attorney may ask some follow-up questions to "rehabilitate" you.

As is always the case, the best way to meet questions about bias is with the truth. The truth is child care professionals and social workers deal with uncooperative and unsavory people nearly every day. It is part of their environment. Professionals quickly learn to make decisions independent of their personal feelings.

Don't expect, however, that opposing counsel will allow much wiggle room in answer to questions during the cross-examination. Rather, you will have to depend on your attorney to rehabilitate you through redirect examination. The questioning could evolve differently:

ATTORNEY: You don't particularly like my client, do you?

SOCIAL WORKER: *I wouldn't necessarily say that.*

ATTORNEY: But the truth is you are not fond of Mr. Jones, wouldn't that be fair to say?

SOCIAL WORKER: *No, but I'm confident that did not impact my decisions, and I'd be more than willing to explain why I'm so confident that bias did not affect my decision, if you're interested.*

ATTORNEY: Your Honor, I ask that the witness's statement be stricken as unresponsive and the jury be advised to disregard it.

> *JUDGE:* *The answer was not entirely responsive. The jury will disregard that portion of the witness's answer after she answered "No."*

While, technically, the witness's response may have been unresponsive, the information the witness wanted to share is material and relevant, thus passing two crucial tests of admissibility. Your attorney, having been alerted to the fact that you have some valuable information to share with the judge and jury, can bring the matter up on redirect examination.

> *YOUR ATTORNEY:* Earlier, you said you were confident your dislike for Mr. Jones did not affect your decisions in this case. How can you be so sure?

> *WITNESS:* *I have worked in this field for eight years. I deal with people who manipulate, insult, abuse or neglect children, disrespect elders and regularly engage in disreputable conduct. It's part of my job. I quickly learned after leaving college and entering the real world of work that you have to put your personal feelings aside if you want to do your job well. Yes, I still care. I care deeply. But I won't permit myself to shade facts or fudge them in order to get a result. I couldn't sleep well at night if I did that. And I didn't do it in this case, either.*

Impeachment by Demonstrating Poor Memory

The tactic of impeachment by showing that the witness has a poor memory is often attempted when opposing counsel is unable to demonstrate bias or prejudice. The witness may have impeccable credentials or a reputation for honesty in the community. Under these circumstances, opposing counsel must attempt other means of impeachment.

Very few people have total recall. To make matters worse, age impairs memory. Psychologists have found that memory operates at peak efficiency when we are about seventeen years old, and it's all downhill after that. We are prone to forget things, and most jurors know this from personal experience. That is why impeachment by demonstrating poor memory is such an effective tactic.

But we shouldn't assume that simply because something happened several months or years ago, it is beyond our ability to recall it. Most baby boomers can recall exactly where they were on November 22, 1963, when President John F. Kennedy was assassinated. Younger generations will probably recall their place when the World Trade Center was destroyed by terrorists on September 11, 2001. Simply because an event is not fresh in time does not mean it is not fresh in memory.

We all have constructs to help us remember things, little mental hooks we use to keep data orderly in our brains. When the triggering fact is brought to the conscious mind, the connected fact surfaces as well. Those triggers can be almost anything: a word, an image, a smell, or even the feel of something. Psychologists have found that our brains do not always make connections when we are anxious. This explains the common occurrence of memory lapse on the witness stand.

People are not necessarily untrustworthy, although some witnesses are. Rather, the drama of the courtroom heightens anxiety and causes some witnesses to freeze up on the stand. That is why good attorneys try to get the witness loosened up by asking "friendly" questions during the first few minutes of direct examination, questions such as: "Are you married?" "Do you have children?" "Tell us their names and how old they are."

Not too surprisingly, some witnesses are so nervous they have trouble with even these easy questions. I can think of several instances when a witness couldn't name his children, much less their ages. A good attorney will have taken the witness to the courtroom and staged a mock direct and cross-examination before trial. With preparation and a relaxed state of mind, the witness will respond appropriately when the time comes to testify.

If you can't remember something while being questioned, a good response is "I cannot remember that at this time." This is important because it allows the jury to infer you suffer from a temporary loss of memory, which jurors have experienced as well, rather than a lack of honesty. If they think you're dishonest, your whole testimony is worth nothing and may actually hurt your side in the case.

Judges almost always tell jurors that if they determine a witness has intentionally lied on the stand, they may reject part or all of the witness's testimony. Consequently, it is important, if you honestly cannot remember something, to say so. If the answer comes to you later, it may be appropriate to say: "Judge, I just remembered the answer to Mr. Smith's question a while back. Can I answer it now?" Most judges will allow this.

By answering, "I cannot remember at this time," the witness gives his attorney the opportunity on redirect to use a mental hook that will release the memory. Though opposing counsel will be quick to criticize this testimony as being made up, jurors know that memories are not ironclad and that the pressure of questioning under oath can cause a little slippage.

Here is an example of a cross-examination using faulty memory as an impeachment tool. The case involves an alleged assault on a victim by a stranger.

ATTORNEY: Was my client wearing a jacket that night?

WITNESS: *I believe so.*

ATTORNEY: What color was it?

WITNESS: *Dark brown or blue, I'm not sure.*

ATTORNEY: Did it have a zipper or was it a pullover?

WITNESS: *I think it had a zipper.*

ATTORNEY: But you're not sure?

PROSECUTOR: *Objection, Your Honor. This is irrelevant.*

ATTORNEY: Your Honor, this goes to the witness's memory and therefore her credibility.

JUDGE: *Overruled. Please answer the question.*

WITNESS: *I'm not sure if it had a zipper.*

ATTORNEY: Was he wearing boots, shoes, or sandals?

WITNESS: *Shoes. I'm sure of that.*

ATTORNEY: What kind of pants was he wearing — blue jeans, dress pants, or something else?

WITNESS: *Dark slacks, that's all I remember.*

ATTORNEY: Was he wearing a T-shirt under his shirt?

WITNESS: *I couldn't say for sure.*

ATTORNEY: Did he have any rings on his hands?

WITNESS: *I don't know.*

ATTORNEY: No further questions.

While your attorney can argue that these memory lapses are inconsequential, the other side will counter that this testimony shows your testimony is flawed. Perhaps this is all it will take to convince one of the jurors that an issue has not been proven satisfactorily. The result? A hung jury. A hung jury is almost as good as a win from the defendant's perspective, because a new trial probably can't be rescheduled in the immediate future.

Time is usually the ally of the defendant, whether the case is criminal or civil in nature. The more time that elapses before trial, the greater the likelihood that witnesses may move away, die, or forget the events in question. Also, in publicized criminal cases, time allows the public furor to subside and anger to diminish. All of this works to the advantage of the defendant.

The best way to counter this impeachment tactic is to write down your observations soon after the incident. Memory is not like wine; it does not improve with age. It is far better to rely on good notes than on your memory.

Impeachment by Demonstrating Lack of Perception

Eyewitnesses are asked to relate in court, events they saw or otherwise sensed. But simply because they witnessed something does not mean their perceptions were necessarily accurate. Studies show that eyewitness identifications are accurate only slightly more than half the time.

Amnesty International and other groups opposed to capital punishment cite several cases where death-row convicts have been exonerated by DNA testing after eyewitnesses convinced jurors of their guilt. Jury trials are highly charged events, and a whole host of factors can influence a verdict. A confident witness who without hesitation positively identifies a defendant under somewhat adverse conditions (poor lighting, short exposure, traumatic circumstances) may be at least as convincing as a less impressive witness who observed someone under ideal conditions.

The job of the cross-examiner is to show the jury that the witness's perception was not accurate. There are a host of ways to do this, but they all rest upon the assumption that what we think we saw wasn't necessarily true.

The attorney may demonstrate that the witness did not see the whole person or event, but only a piece of it. Biases and prejudices may be inquired about, to show that the witness saw what he "wanted" to see. The attorney may ask about the witness's physical state: "How much sleep did you get the night before?" "How much stress were you under the day the incident took place?" "Were you under the influence of any mind-altering substances at the time?"

The attorney may focus on the environment: Was it too bright, too dark, rainy, cloudy, foggy, too hot, or too cold? Anything that might affect the body's ability to effectively function is a likely subject for cross-examination. Additionally, the attorney may inquire about any distractions that might have impaired perception and impediments. "Do you wear glasses?" "What is your vision, uncorrected by glasses or contact lenses?" "Were you wearing sunglasses?" "Do you suffer from tinnitus or any other hearing disorder?"

Some judges will allow attorneys to perform experiments in the courtroom. An attorney may want to test your vision or hearing from the distance you claim to have seen or heard the event in question. This is a good reason to be careful when answering questions about distance. Remember how phrasing of questions can impact your answer. "How loudly did she call out?" may elicit a different response than the question, "Would you describe the tone of her voice when she called out?"

In most cases, the attorney will focus on the element of time to show that a witness's perception was faulty because the glimpse of the subject was fleeting. If the witness had only seconds to observe the event, the attorney will harp on that factor. The attorney is likely to question the witness about other people, objects, or things around the event. Did the witness notice the man behind the defendant? Did the witness notice if the window of the car was open or closed? The point that will be made during closing argument is that the witness's opportunity to correctly observe the event was hampered by the short time involved.

None of this is to imply that a witness should conjure up detail that really is not in the memory bank. Just respond truthfully, but without surprise or dismay.

Impeachment Through Prior Inconsistent Statements

When a witness testifies about facts that are very important to the case, opposing counsel may try to prove that the witness previously made statements inconsistent with the testimony. The intent is not necessarily to show that the earlier statement was true and the more recent statement false but that any witness who is so inconsistent cannot be believed.

There are two methods to impeach through prior inconsistent statements. One is to call another witness to testify that an earlier inconsistent statement was made.

DEFENSE ATTORNEY: Ms. Kramer, you heard Brad Johnson testify today that he thought my client, Mr. Campbell, was drunk on November 8?

WITNESS: *Yes, I did.*

DEFENSE: Have you known Brad Johnson long?

WITNESS: *For about two years.*

DEFENSE: Have you ever talked to him about the incident on November 8?

WITNESS: *Yes, we talked about it a few days after it happened.*

DEFENSE: Back in November?

WITNESS: *Yes.*

DEFENSE: What did Brad Johnson say back then?

WITNESS: *He said Mr. Campbell was a pain in the you-know-what, but he wasn't drunk.*

DEFENSE: Thank you, Ms. Kramer. I have no further questions.

The second method is to have the witness who is being impeached admit the prior inconsistent statement during cross-examination. This method, if done properly, can be dramatic:

ATTORNEY: Ms. Smith, you say that right after the accident you noticed ten feet of skid marks directly behind the location where the defendant's Chevy came to a stop?

WITNESS: *That is correct.*

ATTORNEY: Do you recall giving a deposition in my office last June where we questioned you about this matter?

WITNESS: *Yes, I do.*

ATTORNEY: Do you recall that your attorney was present at the deposition and that a court reporter was taking down everything we said?

WITNESS: *Yes.*

ATTORNEY: You were put under oath, you raised your right hand, and you swore to tell the truth that day, didn't you?

WITNESS: *Yes, I did.*

ATTORNEY: And you told the truth then, didn't you?

WITNESS: *Yes.*

ATTORNEY: At that deposition, I told you up front that if any of my questions were confusing or if you did not understand

a question, you should simply let me know and I would
rephrase it. Do you remember that?

WITNESS: *Yes.*

ATTORNEY: And you told me that you would let me know if you didn't
understand a question, didn't you?

WITNESS: *Yes.*

ATTORNEY: Before you came to my office for that deposition, you
discussed what questions I might ask with your own attorney,
didn't you?

WITNESS: *Yes.*

ATTORNEY: After you gave your answers under oath with your attorney
present, the questions and answers were typed out and given
to you to read to see if they were accurate, right?

WITNESS: *Yes, that's right.*

ATTORNEY: And, in fact, you did read the questions and answers and
you signed the deposition on the last page under oath before
a notary, indicating that everything was accurately recorded,
correct?

WITNESS: *Yes.*

ATTORNEY: Would it be fair to say that your memory of the accident last
June was better and fresher than it is today?

WITNESS: *I suppose so.*

ATTORNEY: Now, Ms. Smith, at your deposition, under oath, with your
attorney present, weren't you asked the following question
and didn't you give the following answer: "Question — After
you arrived at the scene of the accident, did you see any
skid marks? Answer — No, I looked all around but didn't see
any." That's what you said, isn't it?

WITNESS: *If it's in there, I must have said it.*

It is extremely difficult to override impeachment because of a prior inconsistent statement. If you make a statement and later contradict it, you
will likely be impeached. If you were mistaken when you made the earlier
statement, it is probably best to have your attorney bring the matter up
during direct examination in order to take the sting out of the issue. In

other words, your attorney can bring it up first and let you explain why your testimony in court differs from that given at the deposition.

> **YOUR ATTORNEY:** Ms. Smith, today you testified about skid marks you saw at the scene, correct?
>
> **WITNESS:** *Yes.*
>
> **ATTORNEY:** But when you were asked questions during a deposition last June, you told us you did not see any skid marks. Can you explain?
>
> **WITNESS:** *I'm not sure if it was because I was nervous, but I must have forgotten what I did at the scene. I've read that deposition and I was just plain wrong about the skid marks. I'm sorry that I messed that up.*

Most likely, your attorney will have noticed any prior inconsistent statements and will plan with you how to address them during direct examination. If your attorney does not raise the issue with you before trial, you should do so on your own.

Impeachment by Implying That an Opinion Is Wrong

There is an effective method of discrediting a witness who has given an opinion. The jury is informed, through cross-examination, that the witness's views differ from those of leading experts, are out of the mainstream, and by implication are wrong.

For example, if an expert testified that surgery was the appropriate treatment for a patient's malady, opposing counsel will challenge that view with treatises or publications in that field which state that a different treatment would have been more appropriate.

Impeachment by Attacking Character

Probably the least commonly used method of impeaching a witness is by an attack on character. Nevertheless, it is important to know all the tactics the opposition can use to discredit your testimony.

One way to attack character is to show evidence that the witness has been convicted of a crime. This attack is allowed on the theory that criminals, generally, are untrustworthy. The courts in various states have different standards for determining what kinds of crimes are permissible subjects for impeachment purposes. Most do not allow a witness to be impeached with evidence of misdemeanors unless they involve dishonesty or false statement. Almost all courts will permit impeachment by revelation of a felony.

Impeachment through evidence of a criminal conviction is limited in scope. Most courts will allow the impeaching attorney to ask a witness for the name of the crime, the time and place of conviction, and the punishment. Details, such as the name of the victim and any aggravating circumstances, are not admissible, nor are convictions more than ten years old.

Evidence of a witness's criminal record can be introduced through the witness or by documentation. The impeaching attorney usually asks the witness the particulars of the crime, then introduces, as an exhibit, a certified copy of the judgment of conviction.

The use of a witness's prior criminal record to discredit testimony is but one of the reasons why law enforcement agencies screen applicants thoroughly and have a low tolerance for dishonesty on the job. The officer's value to the agency can be greatly compromised by any criminal conviction.

A second method of character impeachment is to demonstrate the witness's reputation for untruthfulness. This is done, not by questioning the witness who is to be impeached but by soliciting testimony from others who know the witness.

ATTORNEY: Ms. Epstein, do you know the general reputation in this community of James Smith for truth and veracity?

WITNESS: *Yes, I do.*

ATTORNEY: What is that reputation?

WITNESS: *It is not very good, I'm afraid.*

The witness is not allowed to recite specific instances of untruthful conduct or to give a personal opinion of Smith's veracity. Only Smith's reputation in the community is admissible, and is limited to his character for truthfulness. The impeachment cannot stray to community reputation for laziness, sexual misconduct or any host of other bad traits.

Some Tips for Testifying on Cross-Examination

Now that you know some of the methods defense attorneys use to discredit witness's testimony, here are some tips for enhancing your credibility in the eyes of the jury and judge.

TIP 33

Do not volunteer any information

> Never say anything on the phone that you wouldn't want
> your mother to hear at your trial. (Advice to women she
> employed in her escort service.)
>
> —Sydney Biddle Barrows, *Mayflower Madam*

Skillful cross-examiners will phrase their questions in such a manner that your answers are limited to "yes," "no" or some other short response. Occasionally, though, opposing counsel will go fishing, assuming that your response will not hurt — and may help — their cause.

At these moments you should be especially cautious. Do not volunteer anything more than necessary in response to the question. Also, be sure you know exactly what the attorney is seeking before you respond. Sometimes attorneys don't know what they are fishing for and simply want to give you an opportunity to help.

OPPOSING COUNSEL: You called for an ambulance soon after you came to the house, correct?

WITNESS: *Yes, that's right.*

OPPOSING COUNSEL: Before you left the house, was there anything else that you observed?

or Did anything else happen before you left to go home?

or What else did you notice about my client?

It is proper, under these circumstances, to say, "I'm not sure I understand what it is you are asking. Could you be more specific?"

If the attorney becomes indignant and demands that you answer the question as initially phrased, you could respond, "Vague questions are hard to answer, but if the court is not pressed for time, I suppose I could spend quite a while telling you what else I observed." Your reference to vague questions is an alert to your attorney that an objection for vagueness may be appropriate. At this point, most judges will sustain an objection to vagueness or themselves ask the attorney to rephrase the question.

You will never persuade opposing counsel of your point of view, so avoid a long, rambling answer. Jurors are looking forward to the next recess. They don't relish listening to more testimony than is necessary, especially when that testimony doesn't seem particularly important. Rambling also carries with it the danger that some small part of the testimony could be used later by the opposition to discredit you.

Don't volunteer information during direct examination, either. You may think that certain knowledge you possess should be heard by the jury despite the fact that your attorney has not asked you for it. Be careful! It is possible the information has been the subject of a pre-trial motion and the judge has ruled that it is inadmissible. If you blurt out this inadmissible information at trial, the defense may ask for a mistrial. Worse, the judge may grant it, and you will be back at square one with a new trial, perhaps months or a year later.

If there is a recess during your testimony, feel free to discuss with your attorney information that hasn't been brought out on the witness stand. It can be covered after the recess. Even if you have finished testifying, you may still point out omitted information to your attorney. It is possible to recall you. But don't flirt with danger by volunteering information on the stand that has not been solicited by your attorney. ■

TIP 34

Keep your options open

Most witnesses are *fact* witnesses, that is, witnesses who tell the jury or judge the details of something they did or observed. Fact witnesses tend to be questioned closely about the activity or observation. If you are a fact witness, be careful not to hem yourself in by saying such things as, "That was all of the conversation," or "Nothing else happened," unless you are absolutely sure of your memory.

There is a tendency to forget certain details. Under prodding, we remember much more than we thought possible. Also, we may never have consciously noted everything that happened at the time. How can we be positive about an event months later, under oath?

It is better to say, "That is all of the conversation I can recall," or "That is all I remember right now about what happened that day." Then, if something comes to mind or is brought to your attention later, you are safe. ■

TIP 35

Clarify, if necessary

Assume you were asked a question earlier by one of the attorneys and you now realize the answer you gave was incorrect. You can wait until you are done testifying and tell your attorney about it at the next recess. He could then ask the court's permission to recall you to the stand.

However, jurors may wonder why the testimony is so important and your attorney may consider it bad strategy to bring it to the court's attention. Also, the judge may not allow you to be recalled to the stand, determining that the testimony is only marginally relevant and would consume too much time to address.

But if you don't clarify the mistake you made, there is the risk that the opposition will learn about it and exploit it. You don't want this to happen. So do what most people do in their conversations: correct the mistake as soon as you realize you have made it. Do it at the end of your answer to a question.

ATTORNEY: When did you talk to Mr. Jones?

WITNESS: *That would have been on March 3. (Turn to the judge) Your Honor, when I was asked a little while ago about where I bought the car, I said it was at Hansen's Ford but I just remembered that I bought it at P.T. Barnum's A-1 Used Cars. I thought you should know that.*

The judge will likely not respond to your "correction" and simply ask the cross-examiner to continue with the next question. The judge or cross-examiner may even cut you off before you finish your correction. But your attorney now knows to address it *before* you leave the witness stand, on redirect examination. For example:

YOUR ATTORNEY: You said something about the place you bought the car?

WITNESS: *Yes, I was mistaken earlier when I said I bought it at Hansen's Ford. That was a different car. The one in question was purchased at P.T. Barnum's A-1 Used Cars.*

Jurors appreciate honesty. When you've made a mistake, admit it candidly and promptly. Your credibility will likely improve in the eyes of the finder-of-fact, whether jury or judge. ■

TIP 36

Stop when there is an objection

Often during cross-examination, your attorney will object to a question put to you by opposing counsel. When this happens, stop! No matter what you were saying or how crucial you believe it is to the case, do not speak further until the judge rules upon the objection.

As a matter of court procedure, the judge must rule upon an objection unless the cross-examiner withdraws the question or the objecting attorney withdraws the objection. Sometimes, one of the attorneys will want to make an argument about the objection outside the hearing of the jury. The judge may call the attorneys up to the bench where the jurors cannot hear. Less frequently, an objection may involve complex legal issues that require more time to resolve. Then the judge may decide to take a recess while the issue is hammered out in chambers.

Unless the judge prohibits it, you may listen to the arguments made during this bench conference. Knowing the concerns may help you answer the question more effectively if the judge overrules the objection. However, jurors may not know that it is proper for you to "eavesdrop" on the bench conference, so try not to make it obvious. ◼

TIP 37

Explain technical terms immediately

Witnesses need to keep in mind that the average juror has a high school education, and many have less than that. When testifying, it is important that your words are clearly understood, so you should only use those terms you are prepared to define immediately. Here are two examples:

ATTORNEY: Ms. Longwell, how did you become involved in this case?

SOCIAL WORKER: *Our office received a 960 report. That is a report of alleged child neglect. We are assigned investigations on a rotational basis. It was my turn, so I was given this case to investigate.*

ATTORNEY: Doctor, where did the bullet enter the body?

PHYSICIAN: *It was fifty centimeters distal from the sternum, or two inches away from the breastbone, here (indicates on herself).*

If you fail to explain terms, the jury may not follow the rest of your testimony. Or worse, they may think you are arrogant for talking over their heads. It is good practice to explain terms by example or analogy. Give this some thought before you get on the stand. A jury can absorb a lot of technical knowledge if it is broken down into digestible parts and explained through examples. ■

TIP 38

Beware of the "isn't it possible" question

While judges should not allow questions that ask the witness to speculate, in practice, many of the "isn't it possible . . ." questions slip through without objection. That means you have to answer. But you can respond with: "I'd like to answer that question but my answer would be a sheer guess." If you want your attorney to make an objection before you answer, you could say: "To answer that, I would have to speculate." This should prompt your attorney's objection and, most likely, a ruling from the judge that you do not have to answer the question. ■

TIP 39

Be careful about questions involving time and distance

A frequent technique employed by the cross-examiner is to suggest distances or times and hope that you will adopt them as your testimony. This can lead to problems later. Often witnesses don't realize they have played into the cross-examiner's hands until final summation when the their testimony is recalled for the jury.

ATTORNEY: Mr. Richards, you say you saw my client's eyes on the night of the accident?

WITNESS: Yes, that's right.

ATTORNEY: How far away from him were you at the time?

WITNESS: I'm not sure.

ATTORNEY: Well, you were far enough away that you weren't hit by anything at the scene, right?

WITNESS: That is correct.

ATTORNEY: So would you say that you were at least 20 feet away?

WITNESS: *I don't know; I suppose so.*

ATTORNEY: Now, was it light or dark out at the time?

The witness wasn't really sure of the distance between him and the defendant and should not have allowed the attorney to push him into answering the way he did. Later, in closing argument, the attorney could argue:

"Ladies and gentlemen of the jury, you heard Mr. Richards testify he was 20 feet away from the two cars when they collided. Ask yourself how likely it is that someone at that great distance could see whether a person's eyes were open or closed, much less whether they were bloodshot or clear. Without binoculars, I submit, it would be impossible to see what Mr. Richards claims to have seen. It's simply not credible. You should disregard his testimony entirely." ■

TIP 40

Pay attention to "buzzwords"

In many cases, the defense hinges on whether the defendant's conduct violated a legal standard or whether he had the necessary state of mind to commit the crime. There are words called "legal terms of art," which have specific meaning in court. These include negligent, intent, willful, due care and reckless. When these words are used in the context of a question from a cross-examining attorney, pay close attention because they go to the very heart of the case. Be sure of your answer before saying anything you may have to qualify or correct later.

ATTORNEY: Ms. Salerno, you're not saying my client was reckless when the cars collided, are you?

WITNESS: *That's not for me to say. All I can tell you is what I saw.*

or

ATTORNEY: Ms. Salerno, you are not implying that my client intentionally refused to pay his child support, are you?

WITNESS: *I can't read his mind, so I can only tell you what I witnessed.*

CHAPTER FOUR

Expert Testimony

How to Give Opinion Testimony

The rules of evidence allow expert witnesses to give an opinion about matters within their areas of expertise. For example, a police officer can give an opinion about whether or not a motorist was under the influence of intoxicating liquor.

Who is an expert? Anyone who — by education, training or experience — possesses information that would help the jury or judge understand the matter at hand. It is not necessary for an expert to have a college degree or even a high school diploma. All that is required is a significant knowledge of the subject at issue in the trial.

Typically, the opinion is elicited during direct examination:

ATTORNEY: Mr. Greff, after you inspected the house at 512 Central Avenue, do you have an opinion as to it's current value?

WITNESS: *Yes, I do.*

ATTORNEY: What is that value, in your opinion?

WITNESS: *I believe it is worth $138,000.*

A good attorney will always ask, "Do you have an opinion?" before asking, "What is your opinion?" So you will have advance notice that the ultimate question is coming. In many trials, this testimony is at the very heart of the case. It will boost credibility if you have planned in advance how you will answer the opinion question.

A typical follow-up question is: "On what do you base your opinion?" This will usually allow you to reiterate portions of your earlier testimony and give support for your opinion. It is also helpful if you plan how you will answer this follow-up question. Your response should be thorough but succinct. Don't bore the jury with a repetition of everything you've previously told them but summarize the facts that point inevitably to the conclusion you reached.

Qualifying the Witness as an Expert

In order for an attorney to use your opinion as evidence in a case, you must be "qualified" as an expert. Qualification is not difficult. The attorney's questions will simply probe your background to show that you know what you're testifying about. Here is an example from a property damage case.

ATTORNEY: Would you tell us your name please?

WITNESS: *Mike White.*

ATTORNEY: Where do you work?

WITNESS: *I'm employed with Scott Realty.*

ATTORNEY: How long have you worked there?

WITNESS: *This is my seventh year.*

ATTORNEY: Did you have any real estate experience before your employment with Scott Realty?

WITNESS: *Yes, I worked for three years with Bianco Realty.*

ATTORNEY: What training have you had?

WITNESS: *I have a Bachelor of Arts degree from Jamestown State College, and I completed a real estate appraisal course at the University of Colorado.*

ATTORNEY: Are you licensed to sell real estate in this state?

WITNESS: *Yes. I took the realtor exam in 1992 and after passing it, received my license.*

ATTORNEY: Over the past several years, have you made appraisals of residential homes in this state?

WITNESS: *Oh, yes.*

ATTORNEY: Could you estimate the number of appraisals you've made?

WITNESS: *It would be in the hundreds.*

ATTORNEY: Did you do an appraisal of the residential home located at 512 Central Avenue in this city?

WITNESS: *Yes, I did.*

ATTORNEY: When did you do your appraisal?

WITNESS: *It was in late October of last year.*

ATTORNEY: How long did it take to conduct your appraisal?

WITNESS: *I visited the property twice, spending about an hour there each time. Then, I did some comparative analysis of similar sales in the neighborhood, which took another two hours. I would estimate the total time at around four hours.*

ATTORNEY: Based on your training, experience and appraisal efforts, do you have an opinion of the current value of the residence at 512 Central Avenue?

WITNESS: *Yes, I do.*

ATTORNEY: What is that opinion?

WITNESS: *I believe it is worth $138,000.*

Although many of the questions in this example are leading, they are usually permitted because they are foundational in nature. That is, they build a foundation for qualifying the witness as an expert in the appraisal of residential dwellings.

Challenging Opinion Testimony

A witness's opinion is just that, an opinion. Even when it comes from the lips of a world-renowned authority in a particular field, it is still only an opinion. *Neither the judge nor the jury is bound to accept the opinion of any witness.* This is true even if the opinion is not contradicted by other experts.

That said, many trials involve a battle of experts. One side brings forth an expert to say that the damage to the building was $40,000. The other side presents its own expert who testifies the damage was only $12,000. The judge or jury hears both sides. But the finder-of-fact does not have to believe one expert or the other. The verdict may award damages greater than or less than the experts' estimates.

Nevertheless, opinion testimony is very important, especially when conveyed effectively by someone with the appropriate training and experience. For this reason, the opposition will instinctively attempt to discredit the opinion.

Here is an example of how opposing counsel may attempt to show the bias of an expert witness in court:

ATTORNEY: Is this the first time you've ever testified in court?

WITNESS: *No, it's not.*

ATTORNEY: Would it be fair to say you testified numerous times before?

WITNESS: *Yes, that would be fair.*

ATTORNEY: Of those times you've testified before, would it also be fair to say that you have typically testified in support of a plaintiff?

WITNESS: *Yes, I'd say that's true.*

ATTORNEY: Are you aware that attorneys who represent plaintiffs keep a list of witnesses like you who can be called to testify in a particular case?

WITNESS: *I wasn't aware of that, no.*

ATTORNEY: But you do get paid for your testimony, don't you?

WITNESS: *I charge a fee for my services, yes.*

ATTORNEY: You get paid quite handsomely?

WITNESS: *I don't know what you mean by handsomely, but I do get paid.*

ATTORNEY: Well, come now. If the average citizen makes $9.50 an hour in this country, you'll admit you are paid considerably better than that?

WITNESS: *Yes, I guess so.*

ATTORNEY: You guess so. How much do you charge for an hour of your services?

WITNESS: *Three hundred dollars an hour.*

ATTORNEY: Whew! More than thirty times the amount an average citizen makes. And I don't suppose the plaintiff's attorneys would keep hiring you if you didn't get results for them, would they?

WITNESS: *I wouldn't know about that.*

ATTORNEY: No further questions.

This style of examination will almost always be permitted. A witness may respond, "I resent the implication" in answer to the questions about witness fees but should expect little sympathy from jurors whose income is comparatively small.

The witness is best advised to remain calm, acknowledging that some people might be suspicious of bias given the questions raised by opposing counsel but that in reality bias played no part in the witness's conduct.

When Not to Give an Opinion

If you are not asked for an opinion, don't give it. If your attorney wants you to give an opinion, the issue will usually be discussed before trial. But it is dangerous to offer an unsolicited opinion unless there is solid evidence already *in the record* to support it.

If you have an opinion based, at least in part, on information which has not been produced at trial, it will be attacked and may be discredited by the opposition. You are best advised not to give an opinion unless you have given the supporting evidence yourself or heard it introduced through other witnesses before you take the stand.

In bench trials, you do not want to offer unsolicited opinions because the judge wants to make the ultimate decision based on facts. In order to make a rational decision, the judge needs facts more than your opinion as to what the facts show. "That's what they pay me to do, " one judge quipped after rendering a verdict contrary to the opinion offered by an expert witness. This is especially true with issues frequently seen in court, such as the fitness of a parent to have custody of a child or the determination of whether a motorist was under the influence of intoxicating beverages. However, judges often defer to an expert's opinion in matters of engineering, architecture, medicine or other areas not routinely heard in court.

CHAPTER FIVE

The Child Witness

Competence to Testify

Every day, in courtrooms across the country, children take the witness stand. Most frequently, children testify in criminal cases, often because they were the victims of crime. Less frequently, children give testimony in divorce cases where parents battle against each other for custody. But, contrary to the belief of many, children can testify in any kind of case.

Rule 601 of the Federal Rules of Evidence provides that everyone is presumed to be a competent witness. No federal court has held that the Constitution places limits on allowing even the youngest child to testify at trial. This rule applies in all United States District Courts, and an identical rule has been adopted by most states. As the rule implies, no one can be prevented from testifying in court simply because of age.

Obviously, a baby cannot testify. But children as young as three years have given testimony. Attorneys who want to keep a child off the witness stand, as, for example, in a child sexual abuse case, often challenge the child's competency. Because of Rule 601, the burden of demonstrating a child's incompetence is on the challenger. The challenging attorney may be allowed to ask preliminary questions of the child. However, in most cases, the judge does the questioning.

What is the judge looking for? Judges focus on two things: The child's understanding of the oath and the ability to convey information. Regarding the oath, a judge wants to know if the child can distinguish between truth and falsity. A judge may ask the child, "If I said that I was wearing a pink robe today, would that be the truth or a lie?" The judge may further inquire, "Will you tell the truth in court today?"

Assuming the child responds appropriately to these preliminary questions, the judge will very likely allow him to be sworn to testify. This is so even though the child may be too young to truly understand what an oath is or what perjury means.

Preparing a Child to Testify

Testifying on the witness stand is often unnerving, even to trial veterans. One can only imagine how much more difficult it may be for a child. In addition to the usual stressors, a child is asked to sit in a big chair in front of adults, speak clearly into a microphone and answer questions from an attorney who makes a living cross-examining witnesses.

I have seen children absolutely freeze up under these conditions. No amount of cajoling or pleading could make them answer even the simplest question.

In most cases, there is little excuse for failing to prepare a child for trial. But preparation of a child witness differs markedly from that of an adult. The most significant difference involves the child's testimony on crucial issues.

For example, if the case is one where the child was a victim of sexual abuse, the adult who is "prepping" him should avoid questioning the child about the actual event. Children are often viewed as the most credible witnesses because of their innocence and naivete. A young child who says she saw "white sticky stuff squirting out of his thing" is believable. The child who says, "He made me stroke his penis," sounds rehearsed.

Many prosecutions have been foiled when the defense demonstrated that a child witness was coached in what to say on the witness stand. Child advocates advise that the fewer adults who question a child about the significant event, the better the testimony will be at trial. But that does not mean the courtroom experience cannot be made much less traumatic for a child.

If a child will be called upon to testify in court, there are several steps which can be taken to help him through the process.

Victim-Witness Advocates

A victim-witness advocate is someone who is paid or volunteers to help victims of crime and court witnesses understand and cope with the legal system. A relatively new phenomenon, victim-witness advocates have become more prevalent with recognition of the adverse impact of domestic violence and child abuse on society.

Victim-witness advocates can be found in all federal trial courts and most state courts. They are invaluable resources and should be contacted immediately upon learning a child may have to testify. They can assist with all of the suggestions which follow.

Familiarizing the Child With the Courtroom

Just as adults are more comfortable in familiar surroundings, children will speak more freely if the environment is not totally unfamiliar to them. Arrange for the child to visit the courtroom, sit on the witness stand, and look around. There is nothing sacred about the courtroom, and it is permissible to let the child sit in the judge's chair or in the jury box as part of the process.

Printed or Visual Materials to Explain Trial Procedures

There is a wealth of information geared for children explaining their role in a trial. The Office for Victims of Crime, U.S. Department of Justice, publishes a children's activity workbook with games and puzzles, *Tell the Truth Workbook with Corky the Court Street Companion.*

Another good resource is *To Tell the Truth,* by Brian Ogawa. The author has created definitions that help a child understand courtroom procedures and terminology. This illustrated book provides valuable information for the child's parents and other caregivers who may be unfamiliar with the courts. Available from Volcano Press at www.volcanopress.com.

A victim-witness advocate may have other pamphlets or video materials that serve the purpose of familiarizing children with courts and testifying.

Meeting With Attorney

The attorney who will be calling the child to testify is likely the one most willing to help orient a child witness to the courtroom. The attorney will be familiar with local practices and can provide accurate information to the child and the child's parents. Ask your attorney whether a parent, victim-witness advocate, relative or friend can accompany the child in the courtroom.

With very young witnesses, some judges have allowed a child to sit in an adult's lap during questioning. And many judges will let a child take a doll or toy to the witness stand if it will make the child feel more at ease. Sometimes, the child can better explain what happened by using a doll or making a drawing. Ask your attorney about these matters. If your attorney has not worked with child witnesses before, ask him to consult with another attorney who has that experience.

Scheduling a Child's Testimony

Efforts should be made to arrange a child's testimony for a time that does not interfere with normal nap or meal times. If the child is very young, ask your attorney if the child can testify early in the day before becoming tired. Ask if testimony can be scheduled so as not to interfere with school field trips, vacations or birthdays.

There is an inverse relationship between the length of trials and the ability to accurately predict when a particular witness will take the witness stand. The longer the trial, the greater the unpredictability. Many, but not all, courts have waiting rooms for witnesses. If unavailable, plan how to pass time while sitting outside the courtroom. If it is a criminal case, the child may be allowed to wait in a prosecutor's office. Bring coloring books or other items to keep the child occupied while waiting to be called into the courtroom.

Physical Comfort

Everything possible should be done to make the child at ease the day of trial. He should be dressed neatly and in comfortable clothes. Courtrooms do not always have the best climate controls, so it is best to dress in layers of clothing.

Reassurance

Remind the child you know she is telling the truth and that you believe her. Simply advise the child to tell the truth and to say "I don't know" if she does not know the answer to a question. After testimony is given, reassure the child that she did well on the witness stand.

CHAPTER SIX

What You Need to Know About Depositions

A deposition is a process in which a witness is required to answer questions under oath outside the courtroom. Almost all depositions are taken well in advance of trial. In the vast majority of criminal cases, neither side will take depositions. But if the defendant has the financial ability, the defense attorney may take the depositions of key witnesses who will testify for the prosecution. In civil cases, depositions of key witnesses are the norm.

There are two reasons for taking depositions. One is to preserve evidence for trial, and the other is for discovery purposes.

A deposition to preserve evidence is taken when a witness cannot, for bona fide reasons, attend a hearing or trial. For example, a terminally ill person may not live to testify at trial. Or both sides can agree that a deposition may be used instead of live testimony at trial. The questions asked and answers given during the deposition may be made part of the record at trial by a reader reciting questions and answers verbatim from a transcript of the deposition.

The more common reason for taking a deposition, especially in civil cases, is for discovery, which is just what it sounds like: the process of finding out before trial what a witness has to say. It allows the opposing party to find out, in advance of trial, what the witness is likely to say on the witness stand. This kind of deposition is rarely used at trial if the witness is there to testify in person, but excerpts from the deposition can be used for impeachment purposes.

The opposing attorney wants to discover everything you know about the case and how you will relate it to a jury. Through a deposition, the attorney can evaluate the strengths and weaknesses of the case, prevent surprises at trial, pin down testimony on particular points, determine if standard tests or procedures were followed and gather favorable information. The attorney can also discover the bias of a witness.

Depositions are generally held in the law office of the attorney who schedules it. Notice of the time, place and date of the deposition is given to the witness by means of a subpoena. This legal order requiring the witness to appear is often signed by the opponent's attorney, not by a judge. This is permissible under court rules.

The attorney may also choose to issue a *subpoena duces tecum,* which not only commands the presence of the witness for the deposition but requires the witness to bring certain documents along to the session. As a general rule, you should not volunteer for a deposition. If there is no subpoena, you do not have to submit to a deposition. Taking a deposition is stressful and time-consuming. It helps the opposition better prepare its case. It also helps opposing counsel plan to impeach the witness by using prior inconsistent statements. (See next section, "How Depositions Are Used at Trial.")

Those present at a deposition include both attorneys, the witness, and a court reporter. The court reporter administers an oath to the witness and then makes a record of everything said. The court reporter also keeps track of any exhibits that are used during the deposition. Sometimes, a paralegal or legal assistant will also attend the deposition. Judges rarely attend depositions. There are exceptions for cases where numerous significant objections to testimony are anticipated, especially in cases involving child witnesses or allegedly confidential information.

Because judges are typically absent from depositions, when an objection to a question is made, there is no immediate ruling to allow or disallow the question. As a practical matter then, the witness answers the question even though an objection has been made. Later, if the matter is significant enough to be brought to the trial judge's attention, the answer may be determined inadmissible. It is permissible for you to look to your attorney for advice when there is an objection to a question. Unless directed by your attorney not to answer a question, you should answer it even though an objection has been raised.

Everything about testifying presented so far also generally holds true for depositions. But there are some additional things to keep in mind.

- *Reschedule the deposition* if it creates a conflict for you. There is nothing sacrosanct about the date and time selected by opposing counsel.

- *Review your records and reports* before the deposition. It is always a good idea to meet with your attorney to discuss the deposition. Ask your attorney what the crucial issues are and if your opinion will likely be solicited. Also ask your attorney if other potential witnesses have been subpoenaed for deposition. If so, determine who they are and, if they have already been deposed, what they have already said. This will give you a good idea of the subjects likely to be focused on by opposing counsel.

- *Be ready to tell what you did to prepare* for the deposition. A standard question asked at depositions is: "What documents did you review and whom did you meet with to prepare for this deposition?" Give an accurate, thorough response to the question. If asked "Is that everything you reviewed?", give yourself some leeway by answering: "That is all that I can think of right now."

- *Do not bring any files or records with you* to the deposition, unless required by *subpoena duces tecum*. Anything you bring is *subject to examination* by opposing counsel, so do not bring anything more than is absolutely necessary. In reviewing your file, you may come across "damaging" memos or other documents. Do not throw these away. While you do not have to bring them to the deposition unless they are requested, it is improper to destroy them. Aside from the serious legal and ethical concerns, if a judge or jury learns that you destroyed evidence, your credibility will suffer immeasurably.

- *Be candid.* If something is asked that is personally embarrassing, answer truthfully and completely. Better that it comes out at the deposition than at trial, when it may be too late to counter it or keep it from becoming an issue. Depositions often involve a fair amount of fishing for information favorable to the angler.

- *Avoid humor.* The setting for a deposition is much less formal than a trial. Witnesses have a tendency to let down their guard at a deposition. This informality may be fostered and encouraged by opposing counsel. There are two dangers lurking for the complacent witness. First, the witness may divulge information that should not have been revealed. Second, humor does not come across well on paper. When a particular passage is read to a jury, words that brought peals of laughter in the attorney's office fall flat in the courtroom.

- *Pause before answering.* Think about the question and gather your thoughts before launching into an answer. This also gives your attorney time to make an objection. The record, unless videotaped, does not reflect short pauses, so it does not hurt to take a little extra time to formulate your response.

- *Beware of opposing counsel's pregnant pause*. At depositions, opposing counsel may ask a vague question, not knowing precise terminology for the question, or may fumble about or pause, *hoping you will fill in the blanks*. This is particularly true if the attorney has not done much background research and is unfamiliar with a subject. Don't help. It's not your job to educate opposing counsel.

- *Don't be obstinate*. While no one wants to concede points unnecessarily, there are times when you can and should overlook minor flaws in a question. You should avoid petty skirmishes, yet make a truthful answer. Arguing over minor details diminishes your credibility.

- *"I don't know"* or "I do not remember at this time" are the most credible answers to questions for which you do not know the answer.

- *Don't volunteer information*. If someone asks "What time is it?" you don't respond by telling how to build a clock. Similarly, at your deposition, don't give more information than is required to honestly answer the question. The more detail you offer, the broader the area opposing counsel will ask about. Unless you have a masochistic bent, you will want the deposition to end as quickly as possible. Giving elaborate answers is a sure-fire way to stretch out a deposition.

- *Take a break*. Some depositions may extend over several hours. It is permissible to ask for, or even to insist upon, a break. During the break do not converse with opposing counsel or anyone associated with them about anything even remotely connected to the case. This includes the inquisitive paralegal who is working for the opposition. Remember, this is not a social occasion.

- *Avoid lengthy statements*. Do not try to convince opposing counsel by engaging in long-winded arguments and explanations intended to persuade. They make you look weak.

- *Never make a comment "off the record."* There may be some preliminary discussion, but the actual deposition begins when the court reporter administers the oath to the witness. From that point forward, every word is recorded and is potential evidence to be used later at trial. Before the deposition, or during a break, opposing counsel may bring up an issue that you are inclined to address. Hold your tongue. Whether or not opposing counsel has done this deliberately or simply as part of social conversation, if your response is helpful to the other side, rest assured it will be brought out "on the record" either during the deposition or at trial.

- *No nods, uh-huhs or um-hmms.* They are not adequate as answers. They do not translate well in print, and there is at least a fair possibility that some of your deposition testimony will be read to a jury at trial.

- *Different rules apply at video depositions.* When you are scheduled for a deposition, the notice will tell you whether or not your testimony will be videotaped. If the notice does not give you this information, ask your attorney. This is important. If this is a videotaped deposition, all of the rules in Chapter Two about dress, appearance and nonverbal communication apply. However, you may use *light* makeup to look less drab to the viewer. Get advice from someone with experience in video. You cannot pause long before answering on videotape without looking unsure of yourself or evasive. This may mean more preparation is necessary before the deposition. Don't chew gum, gnaw on a pen, or do anything else that is distracting. Look straight into the camera and exude confidence and sincerity. If you refer to an exhibit while testifying, be sure it can be seen on camera. You may feel a bit like an actor doing a television commercial, but it will make your testimony clear. Videotaped depositions are more difficult than others. Practice with a camera at home or with your attorney.

- *Good attorneys do not attack witnesses at depositions.* Their goal is to find out as much as they can from the witness, and smart attorneys know a pugnacious approach doesn't further that goal. Do not be surprised if opposing counsel is courteous and gracious during the deposition but turns harassing and sarcastic at trial. This is common. Similarly, the good attorney may not attempt to extract concessions from you at the deposition but may very well do so at trial.

- *Your attorney may ask you very few questions* at the deposition, or none at all, unless this is a deposition to preserve evidence or perpetuate testimony for trial. The only reason for your attorney to ask you questions would be to clarify a matter. Everything else is reserved for trial.

- *Always remain polite.* "Yes, sir" or "Yes, ma'am" are appropriate responses in most parts of the country. Some attorneys will try to provoke you in order to gauge how you will respond at trial. If successful in "pushing your buttons" at the deposition, opposing counsel will probably use the same tactic at trial. Keep your composure, and things will go much better.

- *Review the deposition.* When the attorneys are done questioning you, the court reporter or one of the attorneys will ask if you want to review the deposition for accuracy. Insist on it. While court reporters are generally good at their craft, a single word misunderstood by the court reporter or transcribed inaccurately can have serious repercussions. A copy of the transcript will then be sent to you. Report any errors to your attorney before signing anything.

How Depositions Are Used at Trial

There are two primary ways depositions are used at trial. The first is to refresh the memory of a witness. Stage fright or lapse of time may cause a witness to forget information sought at trial. If a witness testifies that she or he cannot remember in response to a question, the deposition may be referred to for assistance.

The common procedure is for the interrogating attorney to approach the witness, show the witness the relevant portion of the deposition transcript, ask the witness to read it silently, then follow with, "Does that refresh your memory?" If the witness still cannot recall the subject matter, the attorney may offer that portion of the deposition as evidence.

By far the more common use of a deposition at trial is to impeach a witness by demonstrating a prior inconsistent statement. The attorney using the deposition for impeachment purposes is not required to show the deposition to the witness first. If your attorney demands to see it, the judge will so order.

Most attorneys will not allow the witness to read aloud the pertinent excerpt, but will do so themselves. This allows them to add dramatic flair to the presentation of the testimony. If the attorney allows the witness to read the portion, no rule says that the witness must use any particular inflection, speed, or cadence in reading the passage.

CHAPTER SEVEN

How to Improve as a Witness

The whole problem with the world is that fools and
fanatics are always so certain of themselves, but wiser
people so full of doubts.

—Bertrand Russell

We learn from experience. A man never wakes up his
second baby just to see it smile.

—Grace Williams

Ask for Constructive Criticism

If fortune leads you to the witness stand more than once, you can benefit
from your previous experience. Remember that no craft is mastered without time and effort. The more often you are deposed or testify in court, the
less nerve-wracking the experience will be. But anyone who says they do
not get nervous when called to the witness stand is probably fabricating or
heavily medicated. Academy Award-winning actress Helen Hayes, then in
her seventies, was asked if she was nervous on stage after so many years in
theater. She responded, "I still get butterflies, but I've taught them to fly in
formation." Experience will help you put your anxieties in flying formation. Aside from attending the "school of hard knocks," we have reviewed
effective ways to become a star performer.

You can reduce the learning curve if your ego doesn't get in the way. Ask
others for a critique of your performance on the stand. These can include
the attorney who called you as a witness, paralegals, the jurors and the
judge. You may even solicit the opinion of opposing counsel. Anyone else
in the courtroom — a clerk, court reporter or member of the audience
— can give you feedback as well.

Be sensitive to the fact that the case is not over at least until the jury verdict is received. Don't approach a juror or judge before then. With opposing counsel, it may be unwise to ask for a critique until the time for appeal has passed and there is no chance of a retrial.

Make clear to the potential critic that you are asking these questions because you sincerely want to improve your skills, that you have a thick hide and can take any criticism without hard feelings, and that you respect their opinion. What should you ask? Consider the following questions:

- Did I exhibit any annoying habits or mannerisms?

- How was my delivery?

- Was I properly dressed?

- Was there anything about my appearance that stood out in your mind?

- Was I easy to understand?

- Did I use good examples?

- Did I appear to be well prepared?

- Did I appear confident?

- Did I appear to be respectful of the judge?

- Was the attitude I displayed toward the opponent's attorney proper?

- Do you have any suggestions for me to improve as a witness?

Thank them for their time and thoughts. You don't have to change your behavior simply because one critic thinks you should. Take all of the advice, think about it carefully, then glean the best of it and put it to use.

If you cannot find a critic, think about what points were raised during cross-examination. Upon reflection, you may decide to change your standard operating procedures. Every time you testify, you should learn something that will make you a better witness.

It is obvious that to be perceived as trustworthy, you cannot be an imposter. While certain acting skills such as voice projection and conscious use of body language may be a little unnatural for you at first, acquiring those skills does not change the core of your personality. In the end, you have to be yourself. By familiarizing yourself with the information in this book, you will be less anxious and more natural when you take the witness stand. You *will be* a better witness.

Don't Lose Faith

Court trials have evolved from the era when jurors lived close to the defendant and probably had first-hand knowledge of the alleged crime or dispute to our current system in which first-hand knowledge bars you from serving on a jury. In modern trials, prospective jurors who have had experience with the alleged crime or conduct are routinely excused. Attorneys also weed out potential jurors who have strong feelings about the case.

Witnesses who testify before the jury are the people who were present when the crime or incident occurred or have first-hand knowledge of the facts. But jurors are not allowed to ask these witnesses any questions. Jurors in criminal cases cannot ask the one question they most want to ask: "Has the defendant done anything like this before?"

When it is all over, the jurors, who knew nothing about the event, tell those who *were* there (the witnesses), what apparently happened. They do this through their verdict. It is no wonder that mistakes are made and unjust verdicts are returned occasionally.

As a trial judge, I made it a practice to meet with jurors after every trial, not to congratulate or criticize but to thank them for their service and ask if they had any questions. Many trials are highly emotional events, and I found that jurors appreciated the opportunity to talk to an impartial person who had listened to the same evidence they had.

In the course of meetings after a not-guilty verdict, invariably one of the jurors would say, "We think the defendant did it, but the prosecution just didn't prove it beyond a reasonable doubt." There followed a list of the things not satisfactorily proven, questions not asked, and witnesses not called.

As a witness, you must distinguish those factors you can influence (Tips #1 through #41) from those beyond your control. You *can* influence the jury's opinion of your credibility. You *can* prevent embarrassing yourself on the witness stand. You *can* enhance the view the judge and jurors have of you. But you cannot control the presentation of evidence at trial. Nor can you dictate what six or twelve people do once they start deliberating in the jury room.

Do your best, but recognize that you are but one cog in the machinery of justice. The system may not always turn out the right product, but if you have done your job well, there is certainly a better chance that the correct decision will be reached than if you had not. Take pride in having done the best you could and leave it there.

TIP 41

If you are unable to get your attorney to thoroughly prepare you, read this book again. ■

Short History of Trials

Modern disputes are played out every day in thousands of courts across our land. But it was not always this way. Our legal roots go back to England where centuries ago, most disputes were handled by the church courts. In medieval times, people in Europe assumed God would sort out the guilty from the innocent. Punishment was designed to deter others from sinning, while leaving the sinner alive and able to repent. This was often accomplished by severing the hands, feet, or genitals of the sinner.

In those days, populations were sparse and few people traveled. Like life in many small towns today, everyone knew their neighbors. Consequently, it was not difficult to figure out who was guilty in most cases. Sometimes, though, guilt was not clear. In those cases, the Church used the "ordeal" to settle matters. The most common methods of the ordeal were by hot iron, cold water, cursed morsel, and battle.

In the ordeal by hot iron, the accused was made to hold a red-hot iron for a brief time. His hand was wrapped in cloth and inspected three days later. If it was healing, that was evidence from God that he was innocent. If it had begun to fester, he was guilty.

Using cold water, the accused was bound and lowered into a pool on a rope. If he sank, he was innocent and was pulled out, still alive, then set free. If he floated, he was guilty and treated accordingly.

In the ordeal of the cursed morsel, the accused was forced to swallow a piece of dry bread with a feather in it. If he did not choke on the bread, he was proved innocent.

When two people accused each other of crimes or when they disagreed over the ownership of property, ordeal by battle was used, the two fighting to the death. If a woman challenged a man, he was buried waist-deep in the ground as a handicap. Lords could avoid injury or death by hiring someone to fight for them, a "champion" as they came to be called. Two champions might have a sword fight or joust on horseback. The duel, recognized by courts as a permissible means of solving disputes in the United States as late as 1819, was a successor to the ordeal by battle.

In the thirteenth century, the ordeal was replaced with the forerunner of our modern jury. In what was called a "wager of law," someone accused of a crime could bring an "oathhelper" to swear that the defendant was a truthful man. He might then be exonerated. Over the years, a presenting jury, comprising as many as forty-eight men, determined guilt, not on the basis of testimony or evidence, but on the basis of their own knowledge or what they could discover through investigation.

A defendant who objected to a jury trial could be imprisoned or tortured by being made to lie on the ground, his chest loaded with successively heavier weights until he either submitted to trial by jury or died. Many were willing to die rather than submit to jury trial because, if convicted, the accused's land went to the king for a year and a day, and then went to his lord permanently, thus impoverishing his family.

By the mid-1400s, jurors no longer spoke of their own knowledge, but heard witnesses. One hundred years later, the jury operated in roughly the same way it does today, as a group of "peers" who have no personal knowledge of the case. We have parted from the manner in which Europeans conducted trials. Today in several European countries, judges take nearly complete control of litigation. The judge selects the witnesses, questions them, and decides the case.

In our country, the impartiality of the decision maker is preserved by the non-involvement of the judge until trial begins. While attorneys may toil with a case for months and even years before trial, the judge often becomes acquainted for the first time with the facts and issues only at trial. This reduces the bias inherent in the decision-making process.

While there are many who criticize our current jury system, it has developed into a means by which citizens protect themselves from an oppressive government, characterized by overly strict legislation or prosecution.

Glossary

This is not intended to be a comprehensive list of terms. The best legal dictionary is *Black's Law Dictionary*. There are several legal glossaries available on the Internet, including http://dictionary.law.com.

accused: a person charged with a crime.

acquittal: a decision by the judge or jury that the defendant is not guilty.

action: another word for lawsuit. "This action was started by the filing of the summons and complaint."

admission: an out-of-court statement by your adversary that you offer into evidence as an exception to the hearsay rule. It may also be a statement that certain facts are true, made in response to a request from the other side during discovery.

affidavit: a written document in which a person swears under oath that something is true.

affirm: a decision by an appellate court upholding a ruling made by a judge or jury. Also the promise of a witness to tell the truth. Instead of "swearing to tell the truth," one may "affirm under the penalty of perjury to tell the truth."

affirmative defense: an explanation for a defendant's actions that excuses or justifies otherwise criminal behavior. Some common affirmative defenses include self-defense, insanity, duress, and intoxication.

answer: a legal document outlining the response of a defendant to allegations made in the complaint. In a criminal case, the defendant does not file an answer because she or he is presumed innocent.

appeal: a written request to a higher court to modify or reverse the judgment of a lower court. Appellate courts generally accept as true all the facts that the trial judge or jury found to be true, and decide only whether a judge made mistakes in applying the law. If the appellate court decides that a mistake was made which affected the outcome, it will direct the lower court to conduct a new trial. Often, mistakes are deemed "harmless" and the judgment is left alone.

bail (also called "bond"): a sum of money filed with the court by a defendant to assure that she or he will return to court for future proceedings. Courts generally consider three factors in setting bail: the seriousness of the offense, the likelihood the defendant will flee, and the safety of the community.

bailiff: a person appointed by the judge to keep order in the courtroom and to keep others from contacting the jury while jurors deliberate.

bench conference: meeting of the judge and attorneys at the judge's bench or table, outside the hearing of the jurors.

bench trial: a trial without a jury in which the judge decides the case.

bond: same as bail

burden of proof: the obligation of a party to prove something is true. In criminal cases the burden is on the prosecution to prove "beyond a reasonable doubt" the defendant's guilt. In civil cases, the plaintiff must prove entitlement to win by a "preponderance of the evidence," sometimes described as proving it is more likely true than not.

chambers: the judge's office.

civil: that part of the law that encompasses business, contracts, estates, domestic (family) relations, accidents, negligence, statutes, and lawsuits, but not criminal law.

civil action: any lawsuit relating to civil matters rather than criminal prosecution.

complaint: a legal document which outlines the allegations made by the plaintiff against the defendant(s).

contempt of court: behavior in or out of court that violates a court order, or otherwise disrupts or shows disregard for the court. Contempt of court is punishable by fine or imprisonment. Witnesses, attorneys and litigants can be found in contempt for refusing to answer a proper question, to file court papers on time, or to follow local court rules.

continuance: the postponement of a hearing, trial or other scheduled court proceeding. Continuance may be requested by one or both parties, or declared by the judge without consulting them.

criminal complaint: a document which contains the specific allegations of a criminal charge against a defendant; for example, "On June 13, the defendant, Stick E. Fingers, committed Theft of Property when he took a carton of cigarettes from the 7-11 Store without paying for it."

cross-examination: questioning done by the party who did not call the witness to the stand. Cross-examination is characterized by the frequent use of leading questions, questions that suggest a specific answer.

damages: in a lawsuit, the amount of money a party receives as compensation for injury or loss caused by the other party.

defendant: the party against whom a case is brought in court. In a criminal case, the defendant is the person charged with committing an offense. In a civil case, the defendant is the party who is being sued for damages.

deponent: the person who is questioned during a deposition.

deposition: testimony taken under oath before trial, and recorded by a court reporter. Sometimes videotaped, excerpts from the transcript of a deposition can be used as evidence at trial.

direct examination: questioning done by the attorney who calls the witness to the stand.

discovery: the investigation done by the parties before trial. This may consist of interrogatories (a list of written questions), requests for admissions, or depositions. The object of discovery is to discern the strengths and weaknesses of the other side's case.

elements of a crime: the parts or components of an offense which the prosecution must prove beyond a reasonable doubt: for example, the elements for a Driving Under the Influence charge are: 1. The defendant, 2. Drove or was in actual physical control of a motor vehicle, 3. On a public way, 4. While under the influence of alcohol or drugs, 5. On a specific day, 6. Within the boundaries of the city, county, or district over which the court has jurisdiction.

evidence: information presented to a judge or jury designed to convince them of the truth or falsity of key facts. Evidence typically includes testimony of witnesses, documents, photographs, records, videos, and laboratory reports.

exclusionary rule: a court-created rule which disallows use of evidence at trial which was obtained illegally; for example, the drugs found during a warrantless search of a house will not be admitted as evidence in a drug possession trial.

exhibit: an object or document introduced as evidence during a trial.

felony: a serious crime, usually punishable by more than one year imprisonment, as opposed to misdemeanors and infractions, which are less serious offenses. Felonies include murder, rape, burglary, and aggravated assault.

finder-of-fact: the person or persons who will decide the case: the judge in a bench trial, or the jury in a jury trial.

fishing expedition: legal grasping at straws; the use of pre-trial investigation (discovery) or witness questioning in an unfocused attempt to uncover damaging evidence for use against an adversary.

hearsay: an out-of-court statement offered in court to prove the truth of the matter asserted in the statement; for example, "John told me the light at the intersection was green when he entered it."

hearsay rule: a rule of evidence prohibiting consideration of secondhand testimony at a trial. For example, if an eyewitness to an accident later tells another person what she saw, the second person's testimony would normally be excluded from a trial by the hearsay rule. Secondhand testimony is thought to be inherently unreliable because the opposing party has no ability to confront and cross-examine the person who has firsthand knowledge of the event. However, there are many exceptions to the hearsay rule governing situations where courts have concluded that a particular type of hearsay is likely to be reliable. These exceptions include statements by an opposing party that contradict what she has said in court (called "admissions against interest"), business records, the statements of dying people, spontaneous statements (something a person blurts out when excited or startled), and statements about a person's state of mind or future intentions, to name just a few.

hostile witness: a witness who is likely biased against the party represented by the questioner. During direct examination, an attorney is usually not allowed to ask leading questions of her own witness. But if the witness shows open hostility to the interests (or the person) represented by an attorney, that attorney may ask the court to declare the witness "hostile." If the judge so declares, the attorney may ask the witness leading questions.

hung jury: a jury which is unable to reach a verdict. When there is a hung jury, the judge will declare a mistrial. The case can then be tried again before another jury. More frequently, the case is settled by the parties if it is a lawsuit for damages, or resolved by a plea bargain if it involves a criminal charge.

impeach: to discredit a witness's testimony by showing the witness is not believable.

inadmissible evidence: testimony or other evidence that fails to meet court standards governing the types of evidence that can be presented to a judge or jury. When evidence is ruled inadmissible, it is usually because it falls into a category deemed so unreliable that a court should not consider it in deciding a case. For example, hearsay evidence or an expert's opinion that is not based on facts generally accepted in the field, is inadmissible. Evidence may also be declared inadmissible if it will take too long to present or risks inflaming the jury, as might be the case with graphic pictures of a homicide victim. In criminal cases, evidence gathered illegally is commonly ruled inadmissible.

information: a legal document which sets forth the criminal charge against a defendant. In many jurisdictions, an information is used for felonies, while a criminal complaint is used for misdemeanors and infractions.

infraction: a minor violation of the law; for example, careless driving. Infractions are typically punishable only by fine; no jail time may be imposed.

interrogatories: written questions sent by one party in a lawsuit to an opposing party. They are designed to discover key facts about an opponent's case. Interrogatories must be answered, under penalty of perjury. Court rules regulate how, when, and how many interrogatories can be asked.

judgment: a final ruling by the court resolving the key questions in a lawsuit and determining the rights and obligations of the opposing parties. In a criminal case, the judgment is synonymous with the final sentence imposed on the defendant.

jurisdiction: the authority of a court to hear and decide a case. To make a legally valid decision in a case, a court must have both "subject matter jurisdiction" (power to hear the type of case in question, which is granted by state legislatures and Congress) and "personal jurisdiction" (power to make a decision affecting the parties involved in the lawsuit, which a court gets as a result of the parties' actions). The term jurisdiction is also commonly used to define the amount of money a court has the power to award. For example, small claims courts have jurisdiction only to hear cases up to a certain monetary amount, typically $10,000. If a court doesn't have personal jurisdiction over all the parties and the subject matter involved, it "lacks jurisdiction," which means it does not have the power to hear the case and render a decision.

juror: one who sits on a jury. The names of potential jurors are typically generated from lists of motor vehicle drivers and voters. Jury service is a duty, and failure to heed a jury summons is punishable by fine and imprisonment. Jurors receive little compensation for their service.

jury: a group of people selected to apply the law, as stated by the judge, to the facts of a case and to render a decision, called the verdict. Traditionally, an American jury was made up of twelve people who had to arrive at a unanimous decision. But today, in many states, juries in civil cases may be composed of as few as six members and non-unanimous verdicts may be permitted. Most states still require twelve-person, unanimous verdicts for criminal trials of felonies, though misdemeanors may be tried by a six-person jury. Some courts allow jurors to ask questions in writing, especially in civil cases.

jury nullification: a decision by the jury to acquit a defendant who has violated a law that the jury believes is unjust or wrong. Jury nullification has always been an option for juries in England and the United States, although judges will prevent a defense attorney from urging the jury to acquit on this basis. Nullification was evident during the Vietnam war (when selective service protesters were acquitted by juries opposed to the war) and currently appears in criminal cases when the jury disagrees with the punishment — for example, in "three strikes" cases when the jury realizes that conviction of a relatively minor offense will result in lifetime imprisonment. In a much-publicized case from the 1990s, Lorena Bobbit severed her allegedly abusive husband's penis and was charged with assault. The jury accepted her defense of temporary insanity. Observers noted there was little evidence of insanity but thought the jury so disliked the thought of punishing Bobbit, they took whatever avenue was open to them in order to "do justice." In legal circles, this is referred to as "jury nullification" and its roots go back centuries.

jury trial: trial where the ultimate decision, or verdict, is made by a jury of laypersons, not by a judge.

leading question: a question which suggests the answer, for example, "You were at home around 9:30 on the evening of May 3, weren't you?"

liable: legally responsible. For example, a person may be liable for a debt, liable for an accident due to careless behavior, liable for failing to do something required by a contract, or liable for committing a crime. Someone who is found liable for an act or omission must usually pay damages or, if the act was a criminal one, face punishment.

malpractice: the delivery of substandard care or services by an attorney, doctor, dentist, accountant, or other professional. Generally, malpractice occurs when a professional fails to provide the quality of care that should reasonably be expected in the circumstances, with the result that a patient or client is harmed.

Miranda: the decision by the U.S. Supreme Court guaranteeing suspects the right to be free from self-incrimination (you have the right to remain silent . . .).

misdemeanor: a criminal offense less serious than a felony. Misdemeanors are usually punishable by no more than one year in jail and a fine. Examples of misdemeanors include Driving Under the Influence, Simple Assault, and Possession of Drug Paraphernalia.

motion: during a lawsuit, a request to the judge for a decision — called an order or ruling — to resolve procedural or other issues that come up during litigation. For example, after receiving hundreds of irrelevant interrogatories, a party might file a motion asking that the other side be ordered to stop engaging in unduly burdensome discovery. A motion can be made before, during, or after trial. Typically, one party submits a written motion to the court, at which point the other party has the opportunity to file a written response. The court often schedules a hearing where each side delivers a short oral argument. The court then approves or denies the motion. Most motions cannot be appealed until the case is over.

nolo contendere (also called "no contest"): a plea entered by the defendant in response to being charged with a crime. The defendant who pleads nolo contendere neither admits nor denies committing the crime, but agrees there is enough evidence for the prosecution to convict. The defendant pleading nolo contendere is sentenced just as if she or he was found guilty. Usually, this type of plea is entered because it cannot be used as an admission of guilt if a civil case is held after the criminal trial.

non-leading question: a question which does not suggest the answer, for example, "Where were you on the evening of May 3?"

objection: a point of law raised by an attorney who seeks a ruling by the judge.

opposing counsel: attorney for the other party.

overruled: a decision whereby the judge disagrees with the point of law raised by an attorney who made the objection.

pain and suffering: physical or emotional distress resulting from an injury for which a plaintiff can seek compensation in the form of money.

party: a person, corporation, or other legal entity that files a lawsuit (the "plaintiff" or "petitioner") or defends against one (the "defendant" or "respondent"). In a criminal case, the parties are "The State of Pennsylvania" and "John Jones, the defendant."

perjury: a crime committed by a witness who lies about material matters under oath.

plaintiff: the party who brings a case to court; in the criminal law arena, the plaintiff is the governmental body that brings the charges against the defendant.

plea bargain: a negotiation between the defendant and his attorney on one side and the prosecutor on the other, in which the defendant agrees to plead "guilty" or "no contest" to some crimes, in return for reduction of the severity of the charges, dismissal of some of the charges, the prosecutor's willingness to recommend a particular sentence, or some other benefit to the defendant. Sometimes the bargain requires the defendant to reveal information such as location of stolen goods, or the names of others participating in the crime. Reasons for the bargain include a desire to cut down on the number of trials, danger to the defendant of a long term in prison if convicted, and the ability to get information on criminal activity from the defendant.

pro se: a Latin phrase meaning "for himself" or "in one's own behalf." This term denotes a person who represents him or herself in court. Among trial veterans, the defendant in a criminal case acting pro se is derisively referred to as a "self-basting turkey."

prosecutor: a person employed by a governmental body to bring charges and litigate criminal cases.

public defender: a person employed by a governmental body to represent and defend those persons accused of crimes who cannot afford to hire an attorney.

recess: a break in the trial.

record: the total of the trial proceedings, which are transcribed by a court reporter; this is what an appeals court reviews when the decision of a judge or jury is appealed.

redirect examination: a second round of questioning by the attorney who calls the witness to the stand.

rehabilitate: to restore the credibility of a witness in the eyes of the judge and jury.

remand: to send back. For example, the appellate court reversed the conviction and remanded the case to the trial court with instructions to give the defendant a new trial.

rest: what an attorney says to a judge to signal that there are no additional witnesses or evidence to be presented by the party represented by that attorney; for example, "The Plaintiff rests, Your Honor."

self-incrimination: making statements that might expose one to criminal prosecution, now or in the future. The Fifth Amendment to the U.S. Constitution prohibits the government from forcing anyone to provide evidence (as in answering questions) that might lead to the person being prosecuted for a crime.

sequester: keep a witness apart from other witnesses to eliminate influence of other evidence.

sequestration: an order of the judge requiring witnesses to stay out of the courtroom until they've testified; also the order of a judge requiring the jury to stay together until it has reached a verdict.

Statute of Limitations: the time limit within which a lawsuit or criminal charges must be filed. The exact limit varies with the kind of lawsuit, the seriousness of the charge, and the state or federal court in which the action is filed. If the lawsuit or criminal charges are filed too late, the case will be dismissed if the issue is raised.

subpoena (also spelled "subpena"): a court order issued at the request of a party requiring a witness to appear in court.

subpoena duces tecum: a type of subpoena, usually issued at the request of a party, by which a witness is ordered to produce certain documents at a deposition or trial.

summons: a document prepared by the plaintiff and issued by a court informing the defendant that she or he has been sued. The summons requires the defendant to file a response with the court within a given time period or risk losing the case under the terms of a default judgment.

suppress: to keep out. For example, the judge determined the defendant's confession was not voluntary and suppressed it.

sustained: upholding by a judge the point of law raised by an attorney who made an objection.

testify: to provide oral evidence under oath at trial or at a deposition.

thesaurus: a book containing synonyms and antonyms for words.

transcript: a document prepared by a court reporter setting forth the words and activities at a hearing, trial, or deposition.

under oath: testifying after promising to tell the truth under penalty of perjury.

verdict: the decision of the jury or judge.

voir dire: the process of questioning prospective jurors.

witness: one who provides testimony under oath at a trial or deposition.

your attorney: the attorney who has subpoenaed you to testify or the attorney with whom you are most closely aligned.

Endnotes

Chapter 1

[1] Craig Townsend, *Mind Training Tips for Swimmers*, www.swimming
.about.com/recreation/swimming/library/mental_tips/bl_37_mind_
training00.htm.

[2] Jennifer Lawler and David Lignell, *eHow to Become Proficient in the
Martial Arts Through Visualization*, www.ehow.com.

Chapter 2

[3] James Rasicot, *New Techniques for Winning Jury Trials*, AP Publications,
Minneapolis, 1990.

[4] John T. Molloy, *Dress For Success*, Peter H. Wyden, New York, 1975.

[5] Oliver W. Sacks, *The Man Who Mistook His Wife for a Hat: And Other
Clinical Tales,* Harper Perennial, New York, 1990.

[6] Kenji Kitao and S. Kathleen Kitao, *Intercultural Nonverbal
Communication: A Bibliography*, http://ilc2.doshisha.ac.jp/users/kkitao/
library/biblio/nonverb-bib.htm.

[7] Timothy P. Maher, *The Information Needs of Jurors in Complex
Litigation*, www.wolftechnical.com/webfocus/infoneedsjur.pdf.

[8] Rule 612 of the *Federal Rules of Evidence.*

[9] Bonnie Erickson, et al., "Speech Style and Impression Formation in a
Court Setting: The Effects of 'Powerful' and 'Powerless' Speech," *Journal
of Experimental Social Psychology,* 14: 266-79, 1978.

For other fine books by Volcano Press

volcanopress.com

Call or write with questions, comments,
orders or bulk discount inquiries:

800.879.9636
sales@volcanopress.com

Volcano Press
P.O. Box 270
Volcano, CA 95689